IT'S AN OLD

STATE OF MAINE CUSTOM

It's an Old State of Maine Custom

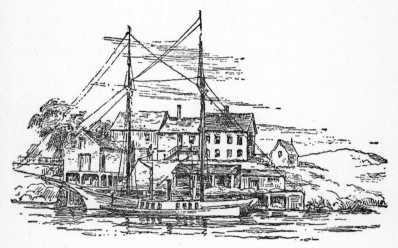

EDWIN VALENTINE MITCHELL

Author of "It's an Old New England Custom," etc.

THE VANGUARD PRESS, INC. · NEW YORK

Copyright, 1949, by Edwin Valentine Mitchell

Published simultaneously in Canada by the
Copp Clark Company, Ltd., Toronto, Canada

No portion of this book may be reprinted in any form without the written
permission of the publisher, except by a reviewer who wishes to quote brief
passages in connection with a review for a newspaper or magazine.

Manufactured in the United States of America
by H. Wolff, New York, N. Y.

To Bob and Anna Addams

ACKNOWLEDGMENTS

Grateful acknowledgment is made to the following persons for their help in the preparation of this book: Dexter W. Hodgdon of Boothbay Harbor, Maine, and Reverend Neal D. Bousfield of the Maine Seacoast Mission, DeWitt Mackenzie of the Associated Press and Bill Geaghan of the *Bangor Daily Commercial*, Thomas McGuire of the Deer Island Granite Corporation and J. Fred Smith of the Bangor and Aroostook Railroad, Charles Campbell, the Portland bookseller, and Arthur Dragon of the Old Corner Bookstore, Boston, Mrs. Cornelius Gardner of West Southport and Miss Muriel Parlin of Old Town, Maine, J. B. Mussey and Herbert J. Salomon, Henry T. Kneeland and Mr. and Mrs. Richard Fox. I am also indebted to the Great Northern Paper Company, the St. Regis Paper Company, and the Maine Development Commission. I wish further to acknowledge the help of F. Ivor D. Avellino and Miss Shirley Barker of the American History Room of the New York Public Library. I am under particularly heavy obligation to my sister, Jean Mitchell Boyd.

E. V. M.

CONTENTS

IT'S AN OLD

STATE OF MAINE CUSTOM

TO FELL THE TREES AND HEW THE TIMBER

DEFLOWERING the virgin forests of Maine began at a very early period. The first sawmill in New England was erected at Berwick in 1631. The amazing stands of towering white pine growing along the coast and up the rivers impressed the early navigators. Tall trees have a definite affinity with tall ships, and the explorers saw in the magnificent forest growth of Maine an inexhaustible supply of masts, spars, bowsprits, and shipbuilding material of all kinds. This was important, because

England was becoming pressed for timber for the Royal Navy. It was not long after the establishment of the first settlements that New England began sending masts to old England.

Samuel Pepys, who was Clerk of the Acts at the Admiralty in London, wrote in his diary on December 3, 1666, "There is also the very good news come of four New England ships come home safe to Falmouth with masts for the King; which is a blessing mighty unexpected, and without which (if for nothing else) we must have failed next year. But God be praised for thus much good fortune, and send us the continuance of His favor in other things!"

Pepys later had the pleasure of showing the King at the dockyard a New England tree measuring thirty-nine inches in diameter, which was being made into a mainmast for the *Royal Sovereign*. Another famous British man-of-war which was equipped with Maine masts was the *Victory*, Nelson's flagship at the battle of Trafalgar. And our own *Constitution* proudly bore Maine sticks. It was in *Old Ironsides*, incidentally, that Commodore Edward Preble of Portland led the successful naval expedition against the pirates of Tripoli.

Maine became known as the Mast Country, and so important were her timber resources regarded by the Lords of the Admiralty that restrictions were placed on cutting the larger pines. By the colonial charter of 1691 all trees having a diameter of twenty-four inches or more, one foot above the ground, were reserved to the Crown for the use of the Royal Navy. A penalty of £100 was imposed for every mast tree taken without a license on land which hitherto had not been privately granted; but the pioneer lumbermen ignored the law and hacked down any trees they chose. A Royal Surveyor of the Woods and four deputies were appointed to enforce the law. They journeyed along the coast and up the rivers marking the King's trees with the broad arrow, the device used to identify government property. The arrow, which was cut into the trunks of the trees, had been adopted from his own coat of arms by a British peer who once served as Quarter Master General. It is still used to mark British army and navy property, including firearms, as well as for the gray prison garb of English criminals.

Marking the trees did not stop the illegal cutting of the big pines, as boards more than twenty-four inches wide came into the market, although the lumberers usually took the precaution of sawing them down to just under the legal limit. To show their resentment against the law, the settlers sabotaged some of the mast pines. The surveyors roamed the woods trying to catch the loggers cutting or tampering with the marked trees, but the frontiersmen were generally too wary to be caught. Historians have noted that, so far as Maine was concerned, the issue of the Revolution began in the forests in the contests of her lumbermen with the King's surveyor.

After a mast tree had been felled, oxen dragged it down to the landing, where it was roughed out and measured. Sometimes twenty or thirty yoke of oxen were needed to move a large mast. The standard of length was that a mast should measure one yard for every inch of the diameter of the butt after the stick had been hewed. The diameter of the butt also determined the price. A mast thirty-six inches thick and one hundred and eight feet long was worth £100. Ships with special ports cut in their sterns to take in the masts were used to transport them. Falmouth, now Portland, was Maine's chief center of the industry prior to the Revolution.

The forest and the sea were the principal sources of profit to the Maine pioneers, and so absorbed did they become in lumbering, fishing, and trading with the Indians for furs that agriculture was neglected, with the result that they were often in danger of starvation. More than once the arrival of a cargo of corn from North Carolina proved a lifesaver. In 1737 Parson Smith of Falmouth wrote in his diary, "There is no wood, little corn; sad complaints everywhere." At such dark times the sea frequently provided sustenance. The parson wrote again in 1741, "The fish have but now struck in; a great relief to people almost perishing." But still the population grew, and trade, especially the lumber trade, increased.

Maine had not only millions of acres of the finest timber lands, but also enjoyed the great natural advantage of having numerous rivers giving access to them. Down these rivers from the forested areas the logs came to the mills along the seaboard, to be converted into deals, planks, boards, shingles, clapboards, laths, staves, pickets, etc., and loaded aboard vessels for shipment to domestic and foreign markets. Eventually the rivers from the Saco eastward to the Saint Croix became scenes of intense logging operations. Important lumbering towns included Brunswick, Bath, Wiscasset, Waldoborough, Bangor, Ellsworth, Machias, and Calais.

All this activity gave rise to another great Maine industry: shipbuilding. Vessels were needed to carry the products of the forests to market, and with the raw materials and other conveniences for shipbuilding at hand, it was inevitable that shipyards should spring up all along the coast. There was also a demand for ships for many other purposes beside the lumber-carrying trade, which the shipyards and the lumberers promptly met, and Maine-built vessels were soon to be found in the world's most distant ports. No better ships were built anywhere. Even when local supplies of the necessary raw materials were at length exhausted and had to be brought from other parts of the country, the skill and experience of the Maine shipwrights still enabled them to produce the best and cheapest vessels in America.

The demand for lumber increased as the country grew. It kept the loggers on the jump. It was the age of big, hard, lusty men, who said in effect that if it was lumber the world wanted, then by the Great Horn Spoon they'd let daylight into the old woods, and cut 'em wide, close, and handsome! And cut them they did. With feverish and intemperate haste they went to work, and it didn't take them long to do the job. They took the choicest trees first —the superb white pines. In a few years they got them all. In the Penobscot River basin, for example, which is approximately one hundred and sixty miles long, with an extreme width of about one hundred miles, the pines were cleaned out between the years 1820 and 1860. The Civil War marked the end of the white pine period of Maine lumbering, and the loggers turned their attention to other trees, notably the spruce, which they had hardly looked at before.

It was during this period that the bearded, hairy-chested logger in the red shirt (he usually wore two), gray pants, boots, and woolen hat was first recognized as a pure strain apart from the ordinary run of men. Here in Maine he began to create those traditions which he took with him and handed on to his followers as the timber line was pursued westward through Pennsylvania and the lake states to the Pacific coast. He played a great part in the development of America, but compared with the enormous literature that has grown up around the cowboy and other pioneering types, relatively little has been written in eulogy of the logger, though he was as colorful as any of them and entitled to as much share in the glory.

After the early lumberers had cut off the most easily accessible tracts of primeval pine, it became necessary to penetrate deeper and deeper into the wilderness in pursuit of the tree. Exploring parties were sent out in advance, generally in the early fall, to locate the best places for carrying on winter operations. Two or three experienced men in a boat would proceed upriver with blankets, provisions, axes, and guns. Paddles were used to propel the boat and setting poles were employed in negotiating rapids. The provisions consisted of salt pork, pilot bread, tea or coffee, and sugar or molasses. A tin dipper, a coffeepot or teakettle, and perhaps a frying pan were the only cooking utensils carried. Thin slices of salt pork were held over the fire on the end of a sharpened stick and during the roasting process were occasionally withdrawn and permitted to drip on a piece of bread. This constituted the scouting party's dinner. Some hardy woodsmen liked to dip salt pork in molasses and eat it raw.

When the timber cruisers, as they were called, had reached a point far up in the interior on some branch of the main river, they hauled the boat ashore and overturned it, and the men set out on foot to explore the region, often cruising the woods for weeks. The white pines were immensely tall, outtopping all others, but the forest growth was so dense that it was impossible to see any great distance, and in order to spot the pines it was necessary to gain some elevation commanding a view of the surrounding territory. If no hill or ridge was available, one of the party climbed a lofty tree. Because its numerous limbs made it easy to ascend, a spruce tree was usually chosen. The lower limbs were reached by cutting a smaller tree and leaning it against the larger one. For a really extensive view a spruce was cut and placed against the trunk of a towering pine. The lookout pointed in the direction in which a community or berth of pines stood, and the compass point was noted by those on the ground; or if the lookout could not be seen from below, he threw down a branch to indicate the direction and a bearing was taken from that.

When a promising stand of timber had been found the trees were closely scrutinized to make sure they were of the right quality. The ground was then gone over to find the best locations for the logging roads, and estimates were made of the distance the logs would have to be hauled. Rough sketch maps were made, and, on returning, permits were obtained from the owners or the state to cut the timber, the usual arrangement calling for payment on a royalty basis at a certain price per thousand feet board measure. The price was governed by the quality of the timber and its location in relation to the waterways down which it would have to be driven.

Somewhat later in the autumn a second expedition took to the woods to build the camp and lay out and clear the main roads. In the language of lumberers, building a road is called "swamping" and the men engaged in the work, "swampers." After an experienced person had blazed the trees where the road was to run, the underbrush was cleared and thrown to one side, and the trees standing in the way were cut close to the ground and removed. The tops of prominent knolls were scraped down and small logs were laid across hollows. Brooks were bridged in the same way. The logging road was not more than ten or twelve feet wide, and beside it ran the path along which the teamster walked—a winding track which dodged around trees and other obstacles. A road over which timber was dragged was sometimes called a "twitch road," and snaking the logs out of the forest was called "twitching."

The camp had to be conveniently situated so that the men would not have to walk too far to work, though a mile or two was not considered too great a distance. Consequently, the site chosen was as close as possible to the center of the field of operations. On a well-drained piece of ground near a good spring, the camp for the men and the hovel for the oxen were erected. The size of the buildings depended on the number of men and six-ox teams to be employed. Spruce logs were generally used because of their straightness and lightness. In a small, single camp the fireplace was at one side; in a double camp it was in the center. In either case it was large enough to accommodate six-foot logs. Firewood was, of course, plentiful and easy to get. The floor of the camp was the bare earth from which the dry turf had been stripped since it was a fire hazard. Huge, hand-riven shingles a yard or more in length and held in place by long poles covered the roof. These were in turn covered with evergreen boughs which, when the snow lay deep upon them, kept the camp snug and warm in zero weather. The chinks in the side walls were stuffed with moss.

The interior of the camp was just one big room marked off for various purposes by poles six inches in diameter laid on the floor. Thus the great common bed which might be anywhere from ten to twenty feet wide was nothing more than a space set off in this way and heaped with sweet-smelling fir, cedar, and hemlock boughs. A vast communal cover was made for the occupants by sewing quilts and blankets together. The men slept with their feet to the fire.

Apart from a few stools, the only camp furniture was the traditional deacon's seat. Every camp had one and it was always called by that name. It was nothing but a long, low bench, perhaps eighteen inches high, extending along the foot of the bed. It was as long as the bed was wide, and was made by hewing a plank from a spruce tree a foot wide and four inches thick and retaining a few stout limbs for legs. It was on the deacon's seat that the men sat before the fire after the day's work and swapped yarns and sang songs.

The songs and stories dealt with such matters as the largest tree and the biggest log, the greatest day's work, the most expert chopper, barker, or swamper, the best team and smartest crew, falls and rapids and river drives, encounters with bear, moose, catamount, and women. In almost every crew was a fiddler or accordionist and a ballad singer with an extensive repertoire of come-all-ye's and other traditional lumberjack songs. Here is an example of one of the songs popular in the logging camps a century ago.

The Logger's Boast

Come, all ye sons of freedom throughout the State of Maine,

Come, all ye gallant lumbermen, and listen to my
strain;
On the banks of the Penobscot, where the rapid
waters flow,
O! we'll range the wild woods over, and a-lumbering
will go;
  And a-lumbering we'll go, so a-lumbering
  will go,
   O! we'll range the wild woods over while
   a-lumbering we go.

When the white frost gilds the valleys, the cold
congeals the flood;
When many men have naught to do to earn their
families' bread;
When the swollen streams are frozen, and the hills
are clad with snow,
O! we'll range the wild woods over, and a-lumbering
we will go;
  And a-lumbering we'll go, so a-lumbering,
  &c.

When you pass through the dense city, and pity
all you meet,
To hear their teeth chattering as they hurry down
the street;
In the red frost-proof flannel we're incased from top
to toe,
While we range the wild woods over, and a-lumbering we go;
  And a-lumbering we'll go, so a-lumbering,
  &c.

You may boast of your gay parties, your pleasures,
and your plays,

And pity us poor lumbermen while dashing in your
    sleighs;
We want no better pastime than to chase the buck
    and doe;
O! we'll range the wild woods over, and a-lumbering
    we will go;
        And a-lumbering we'll go, so a-lumbering,
        &c.

The music of our burnished ax shall make the woods
    resound,
And many a lofty ancient Pine will tumble to the
    ground;
At night, ho! round our good camp-fire we will sing
    while rude winds blow:
O! we'll range the wild woods over while a-lumber-
    ing we go;
        And a-lumbering we'll go, so a-lumbering,
        &c.

When winter's snows are melted, and the ice-bound
    streams are free,
We'll run our logs to market, then haste our friends
    to see;
How kindly true hearts welcome us, our wives and
    children too,
We will spend with these the summer, and once
    more a-lumbering go;
        And a-lumbering we'll go, so a-lumbering
        we will go,
      We will spend with these the summer, and
      once more a-lumbering go.

And when upon the long-hid soil the white Pines
    disappear,

We will cut the other forest trees, and sow whereon
we clear;
Our grain shall wave o'er valley rich, our herds
bedot the hills,
When our feet no more are hurried on to tend the
driving mills;
Then no more a-lumbering go, so no more
a-lumbering go,
When our feet no more are hurried on to
tend the driving mills.

When our youthful days are ended, we will cease
from winter toil,
And each one through the summer warm will till
the virgin soil;
We've enough to eat, to drink, to wear, content
through life to go,
Then we'll tell our wild adventures o'er, and no
more a-lumbering go;
And no more a-lumbering go, so no more
a-lumbering go,
O! we'll tell our wild adventures o'er, and no
more a-lumbering go.

Poker also provided a popular winter night's entertainment. If there were no lamps or candles in the camp, the game was played by the light of pitch-pine knots. It was a pastime that was apt to involve the loss of sleep as well as money. Thoreau, who looked inside a number of abandoned Maine lumber camps, said there was generally a dingy pack of cards left on a log.

saw, and still later by the chain power saw changed American lumbering methods. The old-time Maine lumberjack, skilled beyond anyone to-day in the use of an ax, would be amazed if he could see the speed with which the last great stands of timber on the Pacific coast are attacked and felled. But expert as the pioneer chopper was with his ax, he frequently got hurt. Lumbering was, indeed, an extremely hazardous occupation, and it cost a lot of blood and sweat to keep the logs rolling.

After the choppers came the swampers, in charge of a master swamper whose job it was to clear a way through the woods to the fallen trees. Follow-ing the swampers came the barker, whose special function it was to hew the bark from the portion of the log that was to be dragged over the snow and to help the teamster with the loading. The teamster was one of the most important members of the crew. And lastly came the cook.

The cook stood very high in the lumber camp hierarchy. He was known either as a sizzler or a boiler, depending on whether he was more ad-dicted to the use of a frying pan or a pot in cooking. His popularity depended on his skill in producing well-cooked food from a limited list of supplies. His larder contained molasses, flour, pork, beef, and beans. It was the same salty fare provided on sail-ing vessels, though the loggers were usually able to supplement the camp menu with game and sometimes fish. Moose and deer were tracked down in the snow, and it was not uncommon to stir up a bear. The flesh of a fat young bear was as succulent as fresh pork. Marvelous potpies were made of rabbit and partridge meat. The loggers had special names for some of the things they ate. Dunderjunk was a baked dish of bread, pork, and molasses. Stujo was venison, rabbit, or other meat and potatoes stewed in an iron pot. Black tea was the customary mealtime drink. It was brewed to such strength that it seemed almost possible to get drunk on it.

Thoreau said that a large proportion of the beans raised in Massachusetts were consumed in the lumber camps of Maine. Beans were, indeed, a specialty of the log house in the wilderness. They were baked in a pot placed in a hole dug in the earth beside the fireplace and then covered with live coals and embers. After a strenuous winter day's work in the woods, the loggers could put away unimaginable quantities of beans.

At a stage stop on the Houlton road, fifty-six miles from Bangor, Thoreau was surprised to see on the long dinner table ten or a dozen plates of cake. It was so at all the places he stopped along the road, and at breakfast and supper as well as at dinner. Pie was also featured three times a day. The reason for this, he learned, was that when the lumberers came out of the woods they had a craving for cakes and pies and such sweet things, which were almost unknown in camp. The quantity and quality of the supply, Thoreau added, were sufficient to meet the demand of the hungry loggers, and in addition there was plenty of venison and strong country fare. Lumberjacks were famous for their huge appetites.

The transport drivers who late in the year hauled in supplies for man and beast were called drogers. They did not start out until the rivers, streams, lakes, and swamps were safely frozen and snow covered the ground. Their long sleds, drawn by two, four or six horses, were loaded with enough supplies of hay, grain, flour, beef, pork, and molasses to last through the winter and spring operations. If hay formed part of the load, the droger would burrow into it to sleep when benighted on the road. His horses were belled so they could be found easily in the morning.

Eventually log taverns were established along part of the main routes leading north, so that during the first few days on the road the droger had a place to lodge at night. These taverns were really nothing more than crude bunk houses, but they supplied food and drink and were sociable places, and the teamsters liked to crowd into them. They were strictly winter inns which were closed when the lumbering season was over.

The long trek through the wilderness, perhaps a couple of hundred miles above ship navigation, was over the roughest kind of roads and trails, and whenever possible the drogers took to the ice, following the frozen threads of streams and crossing tightly sealed lakes. Where there were rapids, they had to go ashore to pass them. All kinds of accidents could and did happen on these trips, so it was customary for the drogers to form caravans, perhaps as many as twenty or thirty teams proceeding together for mutual help in case of need. A sudden thaw usually made the going hard and was apt to make the ice dangerous. Many horses were lost by breaking through, especially on rivers where the current was strong. If the break-through was into dead water, a cool-headed droger could usually rescue his horses. But sometimes he could save neither his horses nor himself.

Sunday was always a day of rest and recreation in the logging camps. The men slept late, and apart from the custom of cutting fresh boughs for the bed on the Sabbath, they were free to do whatever they liked. Only the cook and the teamster had duties to perform. One had to feed the crew, the other the cattle. The men usually spent the time making repairs to their personal outfits, mending their red flannel shirts, patching pants, darning socks, mending mittens, greasing and repairing boots, and the like. It was a day on which a man could wash himself and his clothes if he liked, but, truth to tell, he seldom did. Except for removing his outer garments at night, the old-time lumberjack did not as a rule take off his clothes all the time he was in the woods. On the drive down the river, however, he frequently took involuntary icy baths.

For recreation, visits were exchanged with the men in other camps, if there were any in the vicinity. Some men went hunting, or fishing through the ice; other prospected for stands of timber, and still others searched for proper wood for ax helves. White oak and walnut were preferred for this purpose, but in regions where neither of these was available, elm, white ash, rock maple, beech, and sometimes hornbeam or ironwood were used. The men were experts in fashioning ax handles with their knives. Some collected spruce gum, not for themselves—they were tobacco chewers—but for children at home to whom they had promised a supply. In the earlier days of lumbering, it was not unusual for a lumberjack to run a line of traps which he visited on Sunday. Despite the rest and recreation which the day afforded, one gathers that the men were often bored and glad to get back on the job again Monday morning.

The felling or falling of a venerable tree is now generally considered a sad event; the destruction of a clump, a calamity. But in bygone days when vast tracts of forest remained in New England there was no such feeling. Clearing the land was looked upon as a good thing. Whittier in his song dedicated to the lumbermen of Maine wrote:

> Cheerly on the ax of labor
>   Let the sunbeam dance,
> Better than the flash of saber
>   Or the gleam of lance!
> Strike! With every blow is given
>   Freer sun and sky,
> And the long-hid earth to heaven
>   Looks with wond'ring eye.
>
> Loud behind us grows the murmur
>   Of the age to come —
> Clang of smiths, and tread of farmers
>   Bearing harvest home!
> Here her virgin lap with treasures
>   Shall the green earth fill—
> Waving wheat and golden maize-ears
>   Crown each beechen hill.

Cutting down a mighty pine was an exciting affair, and even the most seasoned lumberjack seems to have been thrilled by it. The fall of a great tree made the earth tremble, while the noise of the crash could be heard on a calm winter morning six or eight miles. Astonishing skill was shown by the old-time lumberjack in laying low an ancient pine. He could fell it in any desired direction, even hitting and driving a stake into the ground and at the same time leaving a scarf so smooth that it scarcely showed the mark of the ax blade.

It took experience and a good eye to lay a tree accurately on a particular spot. The method of attack was determined by its position, whether standing on level ground or on a hillside, and whether erect or inclined. The force and direction of the wind had also to be taken into consideration, though a skilled logger, it is said, could fell a tree into the teeth of a head wind. Sometimes a tree would be undercut on one side and brought down by felling another against it. But before chopping a giant tree, a bed for it to fall on had to be prepared, which was done by cutting small trees for bed pieces across which the big one fell. This was to prevent the tree from injuring itself in the fall, particularly if the ground was uneven, and from sinking too deeply into the snow, which hampered the work of removal.

The stands of virgin timber included some remarkably large trees. John S. Springer, who worked as a logger for several years in the Maine woods and wrote the classic book on lumbering in that region, *Forest Life and Forest Trees* (1851), says that the largest pine he saw was one which he cut on a little stream emptying into Jackson Lake in eastern Maine. It was a pumpkin pine with a trunk as straight as a molded candle, measuring six feet in diameter four feet above the ground. It was one hundred and forty-four feet tall and was free of limbs for sixty-five feet. It retained its diameter remarkably well throughout most of its height.

"I was employed about one hour and a quarter in felling it," he says. "The afternoon was beautiful, everything was calm, and to me the circumstances were deeply interesting. After chopping an hour or so, the mighty giant, the growth of centuries, which had withstood the hurricane, and raised itself in peerless majesty above all around, began to tremble under the strokes of a mere insect, as I might appear in comparison with it. My heart palpitated as I occasionally raised my eye to its pinnacle to catch the first indication of its fall. It came down at length with a crash which seemed to shake a hundred acres, while the loud echo rang through the forest, dying away among the distant hills. It had a hollow in the butt about the size of a barrel, and the surface of the stump was sufficiently capacious to allow a yoke of oxen to stand upon it. It made five logs and loaded a six-ox team three times. The butt log was so large that the stream did not float it in the spring, and when the drive was taken down we were obliged to leave it behind, much to our regret and loss. At the boom that log would have been worth fifty dollars."

When Thoreau was at Bangor he was told by a lumber operator that the largest pine belonging to his company, cut the previous winter, scaled forty-five hundred feet in the woods, and was worth ninety dollars at the Bangor boom. For this tree alone they cut a road three and one-half miles long.

As soon as a tree had fallen the barker hacked away the bark on that part of the log which was to be dragged over the snow while the butt rested on the special bobsled used in lumbering operations. Stripping a log in this way made it slide along more easily as it was hauled down to the landing. Because of the enormous weight which rested on the sled, this was always stoutly constructed. The bobsled was originally loaded by means of a heavy skid and chains, one or two yoke of oxen being used to roll one end of the log onto the sled; but later it was found that this could be done more easily with a block and tackle. Once the trunk rested on the sled, it was chained in place, and the oxen were maneuvered into the best position to get the load under way. Three yoke of oxen were generally used, one at the tongue and the other two out ahead as leaders. When all was ready the teamster gave the word. The oxen strained at the chains, half squatting as they threw their weight and strength into the task. Then, with the teamster goading and shouting at them and the sled screaming in every joint, the oxen hauled the load slowly down the winding road.

Whenever possible the trunk of the tree was

taken intact to the landing, where it was cut into shorter lengths ranging from fourteen to thirty feet. Some logs were too big to move in one load and were sawed into short logs at the place where the tree was felled. But logs up to eighty feet long were frequently taken to the landing without cutting. Although timbers intended for masts were often taken down river, it was less work to drive the shorter logs.

Teamsters and their oxen were occasionally killed when a load of logs got out of control. The bobsled sometimes overturned and the logs rolled off, crushing the teamster to death. On a downgrade the bobsled might gather such momentum that the oxen at the tongue could not check it and were run down and killed. One method used to brake a load was to tow the top of a tree from which the limbs had been cut a foot or so from the trunk; these stubby limbs digging into the snow like the flukes of an anchor retarded the progress of the sled. Later a snubbing machine was used which consisted of a series of brake drums mounted on a sled. The sled was secured to a tree and the load eased down the incline. Logging roads were always built to avoid steep grades if possible.

During the infancy of the Maine lumber trade, swamping and loading were largely unnecessary as plenty of pines grew close to the water on the banks of rivers, streams, and lakes. They were cut and rolled into the water or on the ice; but they were, of course, the first to go, and it soon became necessary to load and haul logs far back from the landing. But there was never a grove of pines that was considered too difficult to handle. No matter where they grew there was always a way to get them out. Sometimes when trees were cut high up on a mountainside a dry sluice was built and they were shot down it. These sluices were built of logs, and the great tree trunks came down them with such terrific speed and force that, like the ways of a shipyard at a launching, they sometimes smoked.

The lumbering season was of short duration, lasting only through the three or four months of winter; though as already mentioned, there was a good deal of preliminary work for some of the men to do in the fall, while others were employed for weeks afterward on the spring drive. The time consumed in this last operation depended on the number of logs in the drive, the character of the waterways through which they had to pass, and the distance which they had to be brought downstream.

Working in the woods continued as a rule until warm spring rains and thawing weather made it impossible to haul timber over the snow roads. If the oxen were to be taken back to civilization, instead of being turned loose to shift for themselves until autumn, an early start had to be made before the ice broke up on the lakes and rivers which had to be crossed on the way home. When the long sled had been loaded with everything except what was needed by the men who were remaining behind to get ready for the river drive, the returning members of the crew with the oxen and sled began the southward journey. Breaking camp in the spring was invariably a joyful occasion.

"After several days' travel," Springer writes, "the neighborhood of home is reached; but, before the arrival in town, some little preparations are made by the hands for a triumphant entrée. Accordingly, colors are displayed from tall poles fastened to the sled, and sometimes, also, to the yoke of the oxen, made of handkerchiefs, with streaming pennants floating on the wind, or of strips of red flannel, the remains of a shirt of the same material, while the hats are decorated with liberal strips of ribbon of the same material, and waists sashed with red comforters; their beards being such as a Mohammedan might swear by. Thus attired, they parade the town with all the pomp of a modern caravan. The arrival of a company of these teams, ten or a dozen in number, sometimes amounting to forty or fifty oxen, and nearly as many men, creates no little interest in those thriving towns on the river which owe their existence, growth, and prosperity to the toils and hardships of these same hardy loggers. Each team is an object of special interest and criticism; and, according to the condition of flesh they are found in, so is the praise or discredit of the teamster in command, always making the amount of labor performed and the quality of the keeping furnished an accompanying criterion of judgment. This voluntary review, to the knight of the goad, is fraught with interest, as by the decisions of this review he either maintains, advances, or recedes from his former standing in the profession, and thus it affects not only his pride, but also his purse, as a teamster of repute commands the highest rate of wages."

Loggers believed in strong drink for strong men; and rum, which was plentiful and cheap, was the traditional drink of their calling. A great deal of Maine lumber found its way in one form or another to the West Indies, and the schooners that took it there often brought back cargoes of rum, or molasses which could be distilled into rum. Rum was considered a necessary and important part of the supplies in every camp. Families living along the rivers of Maine often kept hogsheads of it on hand to sell illicitly to the lumberers, who consumed it in staggering quantities. Even temperance advocates sometimes admitted that perhaps the river drivers did need a nip to keep from catching cold. Anyway, it was as easy to get as rolling off a log.

"It would be difficult," said Springer, "to give an exaggerated sketch of the drunken practices among the loggers twenty-five years ago. I recollect matters were carried so far at Milltown, that the loggers would arrest passersby, take them by force, bring them into the toll-house grog-shop, and baptize them by pouring a quart of rum over their heads."

President Timothy Dwight of Yale College called lumbering a dissolute business and the people engaged in it idle tavern haunters devoted to all the baser pursuits of vulgar vice. "Those who are mere lumbermen are almost necessarily poor," he declared. "Their course of life seduces them to prodigality, thoughtlessness of future wants, profaneness, irreligion, immoderate drinking, and other ruinous habits." He might have added that notwithstanding all the toils and dangers of such a life, those who adopted it seemed fond of it.

The convivial spirit which prevailed among these men is reflected in their songs, as witness the following ballad, with its drinking chorus, as sung in the Maine woods and lumber towns more than a hundred years ago:

'Tis when we do go into the woods,
   Drink round, brave boys! drink round,
     brave boys!
'Tis when we do go into the woods,
   Jolly brave boys are we;
'Tis when we do go into the woods,

We look for timber, and that which is good,
   Heigh ho! drink round, brave boys,
     And jolly brave boys are we.

Now when the choppers begin to chop,
   Drink round, &c.,
When the choppers begin to chop,
   Jolly brave boys, &c.;
And when the choppers begin to chop,
They take the sound and leave the rot,
   Heigh ho! drink round, &c.,
     And jolly brave boys, &c.

And when the swampers begin to clear,
   Drink round, &c.,
And when the swampers begin to clear,
   Jolly brave boys, &c.;
And when the swampers begin to clear,
They show the teamster where to steer,
   Heigh ho! drink round, &c.,
     And jolly brave boys, &c.

Then, when we get them on to the stream,
   Drink round, &c.,
Then, when we get them on to the stream,
   Jolly brave boys, &c.;
So, when we get them on to the stream,
We'll knock out the fid and roll them in,
   Heigh ho! drink round, &c.,
     Jolly brave boys, &c.

And when we get them down to the boom,
  Drink round, &c.,
And when we get them down to the boom,
  Jolly brave boys, &c.;
And when we get them down to the boom,
We'll call at the tavern for brandy and rum,
  Heigh ho! drink round, &c.,
    Jolly brave boys, &c.

So when we get them down to the mill,
  'Tis drink round, &c.,
So when we get them down to the mill,
  Jolly brave boys, &c.;
And when we get them down to the mill,
We'll call for the liquor and drink our fill,
  Heigh ho! drink round, &c.,
    Jolly brave boys, &c.

The merchant he takes us by the hand,
  Drink round, brave boys! drink round,
    brave boys!
The merchant he takes us by the hand,
  And jolly brave boys are we;
The merchant he takes us by the hand,
Saying, "Sirs, I have goods at your command";
  But heigh ho! drink round, brave boys,
    The money will foot up a "spree."

According to Joanna Colcord, the songs the lumberjacks sang were called shanteys, because they

were sung in the shanties of the lumber camps, and she suggests that since many of the loggers went to sea during the milder months of the years, taking their music with them, the sea shantey of the days of sail may have derived its name from the so-called shantey of the Maine lumberjacks.

The lot of a policeman in a great lumber port like Bangor could hardly have been a happy one when the loggers and river drivers came to town bent on having a frolic. It was estimated during the middle decades of the last century that ten thousand men were engaged in the lumber industry along the branches and tributaries of the Penobscot, most of whom sooner or later reached Bangor.

The situation was further complicated by the presence of great numbers of men from the shipping tied up along the waterfront, the crews of steamers, ships, barks, barkentines, brigs, and schooners, loading lumber for domestic and foreign ports. The lumberjacks and the old salts exchanged drinks, curses, and blows, and Bangor's Barbary Coast did a roaring trade. A notorious section of sailortown was known as the Devil's Half Acre. It was a plague spot of the worst kind, where trouble was likely to break out at any time.

Bangor, standing at the head of navigation on the Penobscot River, was Maine's leading lumber port. Lumber built the place, and it smelled of pine and spruce boards and cedar shingles. No other tidewater port in the world shipped so much timber in vessels as Bangor. When the ship *S. E. Smith* sailed from Bangor for Liverpool in July, 1862, her cargo, according to George S. Wasson *(Sailing Days on the Penobscot)*, consisted of 1,040,000 feet of lumber, which was the largest cargo cleared during the days of Bangor's lumber prosperity. Exactly a decade later came the record year, when shipments of nearly 250,000,000 feet of long lumber were made.

Under the stimulus of the lumber trade the population of Bangor jumped from 2,800 in 1830 to 8,000 in 1834. Stories of the fortunes made in timber transactions led in 1835 to the wildest speculations in forest lands. The town was overrun with hungry and eager carpetbaggers—gamblers, speculators, and adventurers of every description—all bent on becoming millionaires. Ragged rascals hawked townships about the streets, and swampland not worth much of anything one day sold for larger and larger sums as it rapidly changed hands the next. An amusing item that appeared in *Niles' Register* (Baltimore) in June, 1835, is quoted in the Maine volume of the American Guide Series: "It is rumored that one evening last week, two paupers escaped from the Bangor almshouse, and though they were caught early the next morning, yet in the meantime, before they were secured, they had

made $1800 each by speculating in timber lands."
Few took the trouble to look at the land which they
had purchased, but when they did and saw how
they had been swindled the boom collapsed.

This speculation in Maine timber lands had its
repercussions in other parts of the country. Experienced Yankee lumbermen, for example, dis-
covering that there were vast tracts of pine lands
around the sources of the Allegheny River in Pennsylvania which were not appreciated at their full
value by the few pioneers living in the region, purchased considerable land around the headwaters
of the Redbank and Clarion Rivers. The Yankees
had learned how to estimate the value of pine land
by the tree and by the log, while the Pennsyl-
vanians still reckoned it by the acre. So when the
New Englanders moved in and cut the timber they
reaped a handsome profit. But their invasion stimulated other lumbering operations in the region and
was considered a good thing.

To return to the lumber camp in the Maine
woods where the men left behind were preparing
for the spring drive: Before the river drive began
all logs had to be marked, because on their way
downstream they became mingled with the logs
of other owners, and when the boom was reached
there was no way of telling to whom a log belonged unless it bore some identifying mark. An
unmarked log was a prize that fell to the owners

of the boom. Log marks were like cattle brands and for the owner's protection were registered. Generally the logs were marked as fast as they were accumulated during the winter. The man in charge of the camp landing cut the distinguishing device into the ends with an ax, and as an added safeguard, if the log were a long one, he also marked it in the middle, taking care to cut through the bark into the wood. After marking one end, the log was turned over before marking the other, so that when it was in the water one of the marks would be right side up. These marks took the form of anchors, arrows, triangles, bird tracks, and the like, in endless variety.

The most difficult part of the drive was usually at the upper end, where the streams were narrow and crooked and sometimes without sufficient depth of water to float the logs, in which case dams had to be built. It was also on the upper streams that the logs were most likely to become jammed between the banks in immense masses. River driving was the hardest and most dangerous part of logging, and breaking a log jam the riskiest thing a driver could be called on to do. Sometimes the logs which were holding up the drive were removed one at a time until the key log was reached. It was like playing a gigantic game of jackstraws. At other times the foremost logs were cut away, until suddenly, with a deafening roar, the whole mass, with the accumulated water behind it, rushed downstream, tearing away everything in its path. Many a river driver was killed by failing to get out of the way in time. The more modern way is to dynamite a jam.

In the era when lumbering was an individual enterprise each operator drove his own logs to market. When a drive reached the main stream the logs would often become mixed with those of other drives, in which event the crews combined forces to get the whole lot down to the boom, where the logs were sorted and rafted and taken to the mills. But sometimes one drive followed another and there was a continuous procession of logs and river drivers moving downstream. Springer tells how the crews used to play jokes on one another. If the foremost logs of one drive overtook and became involved with the tail end of the preceding drive, the intruding logs were run aground. A crew of thirty or forty men would take a huge log belonging to the other crew and run it up high and dry on the shore, stand it on end, prop it up, and leave it there, a solitary monolith on the bank. The rear crew, seeing the upended log, would knock away the props and throw it down. A score of pikes would be thrust into its side and the men would shove it on the run perhaps fifteen or twenty rods to the river again, shouting and whooping like a lot of Indians.

The river drivers in calk boots were expert at riding logs. Many had been brought up along the rivers and had learned in boyhood the trick of walking on them and passing from one to another. Like tightrope walking, log navigation is an art in which a slip has consequences. The long pike poles which the men used to shove the logs along helped them to keep their balance. Another indispensable tool of the logger was the peavey, an iron-pointed lever with a loose hanging iron hook near the end, used for canting or turning logs. It is said to have been a Maine invention.

Apart from an occasional icy plunge, the drivers had to work a lot in the cold water, and throughout a drive they were seldom dry. But they did not stop to change their clothes even when they suffered complete immersion; hence the tolerance of tee-totalers to the drinking of these men, who worked from dawn to dark to keep the logs moving.

The river drivers ate four times a day as a rule. Breakfast was at five. There was a second breakfast at ten. This was followed by another meal at two, and they ate again after work at eight. Following the two-o'clock repast the camp was moved down-river as far as the drive was expected to progress that day.

The bateau in which the camping equipment and provisions were carried was called the wangun, sometimes also spelled wangan and wangin, a

name which later came to be applied to the river-
side camp itself. In lumber camps today "wangin
time" is when the company's store, where the men
can buy boots, mittens, and other articles, is open
for business. Experienced watermen handled the
bateau when rapids and difficult passages had to be
negotiated. The wangun's cargo was too precious
to take unnecessary chances with. Once on the
main stream, however, the cook and the cookee or
assistant were entrusted with the management of
the bateau.

Spring freshets were helpful in bringing down
the logs, especially on the smaller streams, but a
rapid rise and fall made work for the men sacking
the rear of the drive, as many logs became stranded
on the banks. Abnormally high water frequently
cost the lumber trade dearly in logs and lumber
washed from booms and wharves and carried down
to the sea. But it benefited the people along the
coast, because if conditions of wind and tide were
right, the beaches were littered with driftwood.
The inhabitants of the coastal islands also made
useful hauls of timber when the rivers ran high, as
did the people of Cape Cod, more than a hundred
miles away.

To the lumberers in the Penobscot River area, it
soon became evident that the individual river drive
was unnecessarily costly, so in 1846 they formed a
co-operative association called the Penobscot Driv-

ing Corporation to handle the whole operation.
The members had one vote for each six-ox or four-
horse team employed. The cost of the drive was
figured out and each member paid his share. The
contract for the drive was usually let out by bid,
but the corporation sometimes named its own master driver. The formation of the association led to
further co-operative action, and lumbering instead
of being largely an individual or partnership enterprise became more or less a co-operative affair.
This continued until the large corporations took
over the industry early in the present century.

There were many booms along the river to
which the logs were driven. The largest was the
main Bangor boom at Old Town which was operated by a company chartered in 1825. Its jurisdiction extended for six miles along the river. By
running boom sticks from island to island and from
pier to pier a vast trap was formed to catch the logs
when they came down in the spring. The boom
master and his men sorted and rafted them together according to ownership as shown by the
marks on the logs and kept a record of the number
of logs belonging to each man. The boom company,
which was responsible for the timber, received so
much per thousand board feet for caring for it. At
the height of the season millions of feet of timber
were held at the boom.

The old Maine custom of felling trees and doing

things with them is still an important industry, but the days of the great log drives are over. Some long lumber is still driven down the Machias River, but most of the timber cut is pulpwood for the paper mills, and this is only four-foot stuff. The tall timber days belong largely to the past as do the tall timber men who made lumbering history. The logger of today does not stand apart; he is no different from his fellows.

A change too has come over the lumber industry, which is conscious of its responsibilities in preventing the decline of forest reserves. The Maine paper mills, which use enormous quantities of spruce, cut it on the self-perpetuating method used in Scandinavia. Only trees over a certain size are taken, leaving the younger growth to mature, so that the same area can be cut again in twenty or thirty years. Some of the largest spruces are left for seed trees. If a contractor undertakes a woods operation, the paper company's scalers look at the ax marks on the butt logs to determine whether trees below size have been cut or not. If undersize, the company will not take them. The trees are chopped down and then sawed, so the butt stick tells the story. Operating in this way, it is not expected that Maine will ever run out of wood.

THE THOUSANDS of islands strewn along the Maine coast are continental islands. All were once part of the mainland or very closely related to it. None apparently rose like Venus independently from the sea, or was "hove up," as they would say in Maine. According to the geologists, these coastal islands were the high spots of a hilly region which during the glacial period was depressed beneath the sea by the monstrous burden of ice which

overlay the land. A period of uplift followed the
recession of the icecap, but the land never fully re-
gained its old level. Only the higher hills rose above
the water to form the profusion of islands we know
today. The old valleys remained submerged, the
smaller ones becoming tidal estuaries, the river
valleys forming the deep-water approaches and
channels of the bays.

Evidence has been found indicating that during
the ice age the land was from two hundred and
forty to two hundred and fifty feet lower than it is
now. On Mount Desert, clays with marine fossils
have been discovered as high as one hundred feet,
and a cave over two hundred feet above sea level
has all the earmarks of having been formed by the
sea. At Isle au Haut, in lower Penobscot Bay, which
rises five hundred and fifty-six feet above the water,
beach gravels have been discovered at the two-
hundred-and-twenty-five-foot level, but not a single
water-worn stone has been found above the two-
hundred-and-fifty-foot line. That the irregularity
of the coast was caused by the sinking of the land
rather than by the disintegrating action of the sea
is evident from the fact that protected coves and
estuaries exhibit the same eccentricities as do those
parts of the coast which are exposed to the full fury
of the ocean waves. The marine border of Maine
possesses, in short, all the characteristics of what
geologists call a drowned coast.

By a political accident the island of Grand Manan at the entrance to the Bay of Fundy is part of Canada, but geographically it is more closely related to Maine than to New Brunswick. A bare six miles of water separates the Northern Head of the island from West Quoddy Head, the easternmost extremity of Maine and the United States, while the nearest point to Grand Manan along the Canadian main shore is more than twice as far away. The Grand Manan Channel, the narrow strait between the island and the Maine coast, where the territorial waters of the United States and Canada meet and blend, is the inside passage for vessels bound to and from the Bay of Fundy and the Saint Croix River ports. The tide sets through it with such velocity that its waters are seldom at peace.

Viewed from the American side, Grand Manan appears to give us the cold shoulder, but as it is a handsome shoulder rather interestingly scarred, nobody minds. The whole western exposure of the island, which trends in a southwesterly direction, presents, indeed, nothing but a series of towering cliffs, ranging from two to four hundred feet in height. These great cliffs extend with scarcely a break the entire length of the island, a distance of sixteen miles, and so sheerly do they rise from the water that it is said an ocean liner could come right alongside almost anywhere.

All the villages of Grand Manan—North Head,

Castalia, Woodward's Cove, Grand Harbour, and Seal Cove—are on the eastern or Bay of Fundy side, where, save toward the Northern and Southern Heads, the coast is generally low and broken, with a number of fine, sandy beaches. On this side is also a screen of small, protective islands, a dozen or fifteen of them, a few of which are inhabited, but not by more than a handful of families altogether. The villages are pleasantly situated and attractive and all are small. The population of Grand Manan has remained more or less static for years. About 2,500 people live on the island, which is a parish of Charlotte County, New Brunswick.

North Head is the principal village. Here the steamer that serves the island docks several times a week, and all supplies for the island pass through this small port. The present steamer is the *Grand Manan II,* but when I first used to visit the island more than forty years ago it was the more brightly named *Aurora,* commanded for many years by Captain John Ingersol, of agreeable memory, who in my youth once permitted me to steer the old New York excursion boat down Passamaquoddy Bay from Saint Andrews to Eastport.

"Keep her on the mark now," he said, "so as not to waste coal."

The run from Eastport to the port of North Head by way of the Lubec Narrows is eighteen miles. In crossing to Grand Manan the steamer bears almost directly for the Northern Head, and, passing close to it, skirts the easterly coast of the island for some distance before reaching port. The passage along this section of the coast, with its formidable walls and flying buttresses, gives most visitors their first close view of the island. It is an awesome introduction.

Near the Northern Head is Ashburton Point, where one winter night many years ago the ship *Lord Ashburton* was wrecked. It was Lord Ashburton, after whom the ship and the headland were named, who negotiated the treaty fixing the international boundary line along our eastern frontier. There is a local tradition that in the negotiations Lord Ashburton outfoxed Daniel Webster, thereby securing Campobello Island, which lies athwart Eastport Harbor, and Grand Manan for Canada. Whatever may be the truth of the matter, the wreck of the *Lord Ashburton* was a grievous disaster in which upwards of a score of seamen perished. By some miracle two or three of the crew managed to scale the cliffs and take refuge in a barn. One of these, John Lawson, a young Norwegian sailor, whose feet were frozen and had to be amputated, afterward opened a cobbler's shop at North Head, where he lived out the balance of his long life, never once leaving the island. One day when I sat with him in his shop he explained to me that what helped him most in getting up the cliffs

at Ashburton Point, a feat any mountaineer might
be proud of, was the fact that his wet mittens froze
to the rocks.

After passing Ashburton Point some curious rock
formations called the Seven Days' Work come into
view. It is a stock cliché to say of almost any island
on the Maine coast that it possesses unusually interesting geological features, which differ from
those of most other islands and may quite possibly
be unique. I have heard this said so often of so
many islands that, with a very low geological I.Q.,
I am frankly skeptical, though less so in the case of
Grand Manan than any of the rest. For the island
exhibits vast surfaces of elderly rocks which make
it look a veritable antique, a museum piece half as
old as time. Similar geological formations doubtless occur elsewhere along the coast, but nowhere
are they so dramatically and favorably revealed.
The stretch of high and precipitous cliffs called the
Seven Days' Work is divided horizontally into
seven distinctly marked courses of rock, one above
the other, like the layers of a cake. Six of these are
said to have been the work of the Lord, while the
seventh or topmost strata, which is irregular, is declared to have been the handiwork of the Devil.

Whale Cove, which opens up just beyond the
Seven Days' Work, is a roomy, partly exposed anchorage large enough to permit a school of whales
to sport on its surface, and with diving depth suffi-

cient to allow considerable underwater play. Whale Cove is the place Champlain anchored when he discovered the island in 1604. At the head of the cove, above the cobblestone beach, is a cluster of white houses, one of which belonged to Willa Cather, who spent many summers on Grand Manan.

The harbor light for the port of North Head stands on a boldly projecting point of rocks called the Swallowtail. The Dalzell family lived at the lighthouse for many years. One can scarcely think of a more dangerous place for children, as there are steep rocks on all sides down which it is easy to tumble. Yet there were twelve children in the family and none seems to have had a bad fall. Since it was impossible in such a rocky place to use a baby carriage none of the dozen children raised "on the rock" ever had a ride in one. Once when somebody asked Mr. Dalzell how he was, he said, "I'm feeling lonesome. Johnny went to Saint John, and I miss him." Johnny's absence left only eleven children to keep the lighthouse keeper company.

There was a tragedy at Swallowtail after the Dalzells left the rock. In 1909 a newly married couple went to lighthouse keeping at Southern Head. Even then it was the ambition of the girl some day to live at Swallowtail. But she and her husband remained at the lighthouse at the other end of the island for more than twenty years. When at last they were told that they were to be transferred to Swallowtail, she was delighted, but she did not enjoy her new home very long. One day at sunset while her husband was away she went up into the tower to light the lamp. Nobody knows what happened, but in some way her clothing caught fire, and she was burned to death in the lighthouse.

The historic hotel at North Head stands at the head of a lane leading up from the old steamboat wharf. When Captain James Pettes retired from the sea he bought the Marble Ridge Hotel and turned innkeeper. People used to say that the name Marble Ridge was a perfect description of the beds in the old hotel. Captain Pettes, I am sure, did not change them, but he did alter the name. He called it the Marathon House, and on the stationery supplied to guests was this quotation from Byron's "Isles of Greece":

> The mountains look on Marathon,
> And Marathon looks on the sea.

Applying these lines to the ancient hostelry was taking a certain poetic license, as there are no mountains on Grand Manan. But the ground does rise slightly behind the hotel, and from its front windows and piazzas one has a view out over the roofs and wharves of the village to the harbor, to the outlying islands, and to the Bay of Fundy beyond.

Captain Pettes was a tall, square-rigged man

with blue eyes and a beard that sprouted from his chin, a typical old-time, down-East skipper. He wore leather boots and when there was a storm he stood watch all night to see that everything remained battened down and shipshape around the hotel. He paced the veranda as he would the deck of a ship, a habit which he probably brought home from the sea. He had been engaged in the West India trade in the days of sail. He ran one of the first cargoes of bananas from Cuba to New York. Bananas were a risky cargo then as there was no refrigeration, and if a vessel was unduly becalmed, there was danger that the fruit would spoil. On one voyage the cook ate so many bananas they made him sick, and the port authorities, fearful of yellow fever, quarantined the vessel and the whole cargo perished while they lay at anchor.

"I don't know why I didn't heave the son of a sea cook overboard," said Captain Pettes.

On another voyage, while lying in his berth one Sunday afternoon, a tarantula crawled across his chest. As soon as he dared move he flung himself from the berth, but the tarantula had disappeared and was never found. Knowing the spider was somewhere on board made everyone uncomfortable, Captain Pettes said. He told many stories of his sea experiences—of encountering hurricanes and a fairly close acquaintance with a waterspout.

No less interesting than Captain Pettes' own

stories were those in his library, a small room behind the hotel parlor. It was a nautical library,
composed mostly of books of voyages and travels
and works on navigation. The latter were over my
head, but many of the others held me spellbound.
No rainy day was ever dull at the Marathon House
during the proprietorship of Captain Pettes.

An annual event at North Head to which everybody looked forward was the arrival of the cherry
boat from Bear River, Nova Scotia, with a cargo of
fruit from the famous cherry country of the Anna-
polis Basin. People flocked down to the wharf to
buy cherries, and business was as lively as at a
pushcart market in a city street on a Saturday
night. As Grand Manan has great ups and downs
of tide, the cherry boat was either within easy trading reach of the wharf or grounded out twenty feet
below at the foot of the ladder.

At the southwestern end of the island is one of
the great natural wonders of Grand Manan. On the
headland is a lighthouse and by following a path
along the top of the cliffs for a short distance you
can look down on the Southern Cross. A pedestal
of rock rising from the water is surmounted by a
natural stone cross. It is a remarkable formation
which is so reminiscent of the old-fashioned litho-
graphs of the Rock Ages as to give the impression
of nature imitating art.

The face of the cliffs at Southern Head used to

be covered with sea gull nests. It was a safe place for them as the only way anyone could get at them was to be lowered on a rope from the top of the cliffs. The Passamaquoddy Indians from the reservation at Point Pleasant above Eastport used to visit Grand Manan in their canoes and gather hundreds of gulls' eggs from the small islands along the eastern side. When they arrived they would smash all the eggs in a rookery, and any they found after that they knew were freshly laid. Gulls' eggs have a very fishy taste.

The most striking natural feature of Grand Manan is the great range of cliffs hundreds of feet high which, as already mentioned, extend the length of the western side of the island from Northern Head to Southern Head. Practically the only break in this wall is a scarcely noticeable niche in the cliffs about a third of the way down the island called Dark Harbor, which is really not a harbor at all, since the sea has sealed it off by throwing up across the entrance a barrier of gray, white, and blue cobblestones. This natural breakwater, according to island tradition, was formed in a single night. There is no settlement at Dark Harbor, only a fish weir and a few fishermen's shacks, where not long ago a pair of bearded hermits lived, whose spirits do not seem to have been crushed by the overhanging cliffs. It is a lonesome place full of ghostly echoes, but worth visiting.

It is reached by taking the main road which runs down the easterly side of Grand Manan—"down along," as the natives say—and turning off on the only road that cuts across the island from east to west. At its widest point the island has a breadth of six miles. The dirt road onto which you turn is five miles long and leads directly to Dark Harbor. It brings you out well up on the northern side of the harbor, where through the trees you get a glimpse of the harbor itself far below. Here the way becomes so rough and the descent so steep that it is necessary to proceed on foot. On reaching the harbor you perceive at once that it was well named. Behind the sea wall is a deep, dark pool of water from which the land rises abruptly to a height of three or four hundred feet. The tree-covered precipices keep the place in a state of almost perpetual twilight; Dark Harbor actually is dark. Visitors are always impressed with its grandeur, but most of all, I believe, by its strange and remarkable dimness.

Like Grand Manan, Campobello Island, which lies just across the roadstead from Eastport and landlocks both that port and Lubec, is Canadian soil. It had many summer visitors in the gay nineties, who liked the ocean and found the island a good place for riding, driving, and sailing. There were two fashionable hotels there then with Welsh names, the Tyn-y-coed and the Tyn-y-mae, the former meaning the house in the woods, the latter the house in the fields. There was a landing on the shore below the Tyn-y-coed, where the Grand Manan steamer and the small Lubec and Eastport ferries touched. The hotels are no longer standing, but the large, comfortable summer homes remain, including the red-roofed Roosevelt place. Formerly, yachts were moored off the island, and in the bay the youthful Franklin Delano Roosevelt used to sail.

President Roosevelt had a soft spot in his heart for islands. Cordell Hull has told in his memoirs how the President wanted to have the Council of the United Nations hold its meetings alternately on an island in the Atlantic and on one in the Pacific. He had in mind one of the Azores and one of the Hawaiian group. He thought that to meet in such places would bring the benefit of detachment from the world and freedom from outside pressure. "Being a naval man at heart," says Mr. Hull, "he liked the perspective obtained from surveying the world from an island out at sea."

All this region was once part of Acadia, the romantic name given to the territories granted by Henry IV of France to Chevalier de Monts in 1603. It included Nova Scotia, New Brunswick, and that part of Maine east of the Kennebec or the Penobscot, depending on whether France found it convenient to claim one or the other river as the west-

ern limit of her Atlantic territories. Francis Parkman has described ancient Acadia in a passage
which is worth quoting, if only as a purple patch
in the best manner of the old school of historical
writing.

"Rude as it was Acadia had its charms, and it has
them still: in its wilderness of woods and its wilderness of waves; the rocky ramparts that guard its
coasts; its deep, still bays and foaming headlands;
the towering cliffs of the Grand Manan; the innumerable islands that cluster about Penobscot Bay
and the romantic highlands of Mount Desert, down
whose gorges the sea-fog rolls like an invading host,
while the spires of fir-trees pierce the surging va-
pors like lances in the smoke of battle."

In June, 1604, de Monts established a settlement
on what is now Dochet's Island in the Saint Croix
River, six miles above the entrance. The geogra-
pher of the expedition was Samuel de Champlain,
who in September explored the coast to the westward, passing a great island concerning which he
remarked, "I have called it the Isle of Monts
Déserts." Soon after he sighted another high island
at the entrance to Penobscot Bay to which he gave
the name Isle au Haut. Both names have adhered
to these islands. The Saint Croix settlement was
abandoned in 1606, after the colonists had endured
the hardships of two winters on the island and
many of the company had died.

The French made several attempts to settle
Mount Desert. In 1612 the island was granted to
Madame de Guercheville, a pious lady of the
French court, who sent out an expedition commanded by La Saussaye. There were about thirty
persons in the party, including two Jesuits, but in
the summer of 1613 Samuel Argall, Governor of
Virginia, attacked them and drove them out. In
1688 Louis XIV granted the island to Antoine de
la Mothe Cadillac, the founder of Detroit, in recognition of his services in Canada and Louisiana; but
in 1713, after France ceded the territory to England, he abandoned all effort to hold it. In 1762
Massachusetts made a gift of the island to Governor
Francis Bernard, but he lost it at the time of the
Revolution, though afterward half of it was
granted to his son, who had remained in America
during the war. The other half was given by Massachusetts to Madame Thérèse de Gregoire, the
granddaughter of Cadillac, not because she had
any legitimate claim to it, but because Lafayette
requested it. She settled on the island and lived
there the rest of her life.

Considering that Mount Desert is the most beautiful island on the American coast, it is strange that
the first permanent settlement was not made until
1761, when Abraham Somes and James Richard-
son went there. For many years it was apparently
considered the Ultima Thule of New England, peo-

ple generally not realizing that here was a superb island sixteen miles long and twelve wide, with more than a dozen eminences, the tallest rising to a height of 1,552 feet above the water—an island with a number of small lakes or ponds nestling among the hills, a place with good harbors, and an arm of the sea extending through the mountain ranges to the heart of the island.

The great natural beauty of the place, with its red granite and gray granite rocks, was known and appreciated by some of the best of the early American artists. Thomas Doughty (1793-1856), the forerunner of the American landscape school, was here as early as 1833, blazing the way for the artists of the Hudson River school, Cole and Church and others.

Then suddenly people realized it was not like Labrador, which the early fishermen said was the place to which Cain had been banished, but that it was all it was painted to be, and the boom started which made Bar Harbor a fashionable resort.

Many of the old summer places were destroyed by the forest fire in the fall of 1947, and only one or two have been replaced, but the fire did not get them all and the year-round places which were destroyed have been rebuilt. The fire did not ravage the whole island, only a belt five or six miles wide near Bar Harbor. So Mount Desert does not look so bad. In the spring of 1948 all the ferns came up again as they always had, even in the most severely burned areas.

Penobscot Bay is the largest and most important inlet of the sea on the coast of Maine. From the entrance to the mouth of the Penobscot River the bay is twenty-eight miles long, and from Isle au Haut to Whitehead Island in the lower bay it is twenty miles wide. Its shores are marked by numerous harbors, including Rockland, Rockport, Camden, Belfast, and Castine. With the background of the Camden hills looking out over the island-studded bay, it is a place of matchless beauty.

This is the region where Edna St. Vincent Millay was born and spent her girlhood. It is the place where she said she was happy all day long. When she was eighteen and a senior in the Camden high school she wrote *Renascence,* the sustained and powerful lyric of mystical experience that is considered a masterpiece. In the poem she speaks of the Camden hills and the islands visible in the bay— "three long mountains and a wood" and "three islands in a bay." It is impossible not to think that her surroundings were a genuine inspiration to her.

That she was also interested in islands seems certain. When she was seventeen she visited Matinicus, one of the group of islands off the entrance to Penobscot Bay, and like all people who visit that offshore plantation she was greatly taken with it. On her return she wrote a sonnet about the island which was published in the local paper in September, 1913. In it she tells how on a salty autumn day when things were not to her liking she thought how the tide came pounding in at Matinicus and of the island women standing in their dismantled gardens, with slapping skirts and dahlia tubers dripping from their hands, gazing out across the water where the men had gone.

Edna St. Vincent Millay has not had to content herself with dreaming about an island. She owns one. It is called Ragged Island. There is an island of that name near Matinicus, but the poet's island is one of the Casco Bay congregation. It is on the easterly fringe of that group, near Cape Small, remote and isolated.

Monhegan Island, which lies nine miles out at sea, is nothing but a great rock rising abruptly from deep water like a whale's back, though it is not bare. The soil is good but rocky. The island is not quite a mile and a half long by about a mile wide and one hundred and sixty feet high. Close beside it on the west is its satellite, Manana, a huge, bare rock that looks like a burned-out star. The steep-sided, narrow roadstead between the two is Monhegan Harbor, which is protected to the northward by a ledge making out from Manana, but is exposed to the southward. It is not a good place to ride out a storm. In heavy weather the mail boat is often unable to land at the wharf.

The fog which sometimes enshrouds the island is symbolic of its early history. Nobody knows for certain who the first European visitors were, nor when they came. In a gully on top of Manana near the fog signal station and radio beacon is an inscription on a rock which some people believe was made by the Norsemen centuries before the time of Columbus. It is a row of cuneiform marks about six inches high and four feet long. The inscription has been known for a century or more, but no one has ever succeeded in deciphering it. The wedge-shaped marks, which are shallowly carved, may have been made with a chisel and hammer, but this is not so obvious that I would be willing to swear to it.

Similar inscriptions have been discovered at different places along the coast—at Popham at the mouth of the Kennebec, and on Outer Heron Island off the entrance to the Damariscotta River. The inscription at Outer Heron was discovered by Charles Pinkham, a lobster fisherman of Boothbay Harbor, who told me he first noticed the writing while on his way to a well on the island. The marks, which he is sure are not natural, but were made by man, are on a ledge perhaps fifteen feet long. He said they could be seen best on a dark, wet day.

On May 18, 1605, George Weymouth in the ship *Archangel* anchored at Monhegan. In the afternoon he went ashore, and while his men loaded the ship's boat with wood, he looked about briefly. He found it to be a fine, woody island grown with fir, birch, oak, and beech, and near the shore with strawberries, gooseberries, wild peas, and wild rosebushes. He called the island Saint George, a name which has survived in the Saint George's Islands, six miles to the northeast at the entrance to the Saint George's River. The *Archangel* remained at anchor at Monhegan that night, but Weymouth doubted the security of the harbor, and the next day moved nearer the mainland. It is believed he anchored at what is now George's Harbor, which he called Pentecost Harbor, between Allen, Benner, and Davis Islands in the Saint George's group. At all events, there is a monument commemorating the event on Allen Island, where he is supposed to have erected a cross.

Landing at Pemaquid, Weymouth traded with the Indians, whom he impressed and mystified by causing the blade of his sword to be touched with the loadstone and then picking up needles and knives with the weapon. When he saw that his feigned friendship had thrown the Indians completely off their guard, he treacherously seized five of them, though they struggled manfully. It took six Englishmen to make prisoners of two unarmed Indians. The five captives were taken on board the *Archangel*, and their appearance in England caused a sensation.

Weymouth's perfidy has been justified on two grounds: that he wished to Christianize the unfortunate savages, and also as a publicity stunt drawing attention to New England. Sir Ferdinando Gorges declared that the incident of the kidnaping first gave him the idea of colonizing New England. One of the savages returned to Pemaquid the following year, and another came over with the Popham expedition. Some of the others may also have found their way back. But this and similar acts of treachery by the whites did not help in gaining the good will and friendship of the Indians.

On August 29, 1607, the Popham colonists bound for the Kennebec landed at Monhegan, and Richard Seymour, the chaplain, preached the first English sermon delivered in America. The service was one of thanksgiving but whether it was followed by a thanksgiving dinner is not known. Technically, however, Monhegan can rightfully claim to have been the scene of the first thanksgiving in New England.

The next visitor to Monhegan, save perhaps for some itinerant fishermen, was Captain John Smith, who came in 1614. On his map he labeled Monhegan "Barty Isle." While it was not permanently settled until 1622, vessels put in here to catch and cure fish, trade with the Indians in the vicinity, and take in supplies of wood and water. It was by far the most important New England island. In

1618-1619 some mutineers from a crew sent out by Sir Ferdinando Gorges spent the winter here. Abraham Jennens bought the island in 1622, but four years later sold it to two Bristol merchants, Robert Aldworth and Gyles Elbridge, who sent Abraham Shurt over to negotiate for its purchase. Shurt got it for £50. Jennens' trade goods and a "parcel of goats" were sold to Bradford and Winslow, who came from Plymouth in an open boat. Shurt made his headquarters on the mainland at Pemaquid, and Monhegan seems for a while to have been deserted. For short spells it was a pirate hangout. During King Philip's War it was depopulated, though one would have thought that with its cliffs and bold shores and nine-mile-wide moat of salt water separating it from the mainland, it would have been easy to defend against the Indians. It was resettled shortly after the war.

One of the most exciting events in the history of the island was the desperate naval action fought near Monhegan between the American brig *Enterprise* and the British brig *Boxer* on September 5, 1814. It was a challenge fight with crashing broadsides at short range. The ships were evenly matched in men and guns. Lieutenant William Burrows was commander of the *Enterprise*, Captain Samuel Blythe of the *Boxer*. Both men lost their lives in the fight, as did many of the crews of the two ships. Burrows and Blythe had been looking for each other, and finally came to close quarters between Pemaquid Point and Monhegan on a quiet Sunday afternoon. The islanders, who were watching anxiously, were kept in suspense until the fight was over, because after the first exchange of broadsides the ships were so wreathed in smoke that nothing could be seen but the flashes of the guns. The fight was concluded in forty minutes. The cannonading died away and when the smoke cleared it was seen that the *Enterprise* had won. She took the *Boxer* into Portland, where the two commanders were buried with equal honors side by side.

The lighthouse at Monhegan is not near the water, but stands high up in the center of the island, where its flashing white light can sweep the whole horizon. The present gray granite tower was erected in 1850, replacing the first lighthouse built in 1824.

Monhegan has a year-round population of about a hundred. Most of the men are engaged in fishing. There is also a summer population, including a number of artists. Early in his career Rockwell Kent lived on the island, and one of his Monhegan paintings, "Winter," hangs in the Metropolitan Museum of Art in New York.

Monhegan is the outpost of Muscongus Bay, on the westerly side of which stretches Maine's lost island. This is Muscongus Island, always spoken of locally as Loud's Island. The story is that during an official survey it was overlooked and left off the map. With so many islands clustered along the seaboard, it is perhaps not surprising that one should have been passed by unnoticed, though Loud's Island is no Lilliputian. It is four miles long and a mile wide. It is an attractive, wooded island, the reputed home and burial place of Samoset, the friendly Indian who made the historic remark, "Welcome, Englishmen," to the Pilgrims at Plymouth. Living on the island in 1940 were sixty-three people, six cows, three dogs, and one horse. Most of the Maine coast islands lost population during World War II, but in many places the fishermen have done well during the past few years, and many are returning.

It seems to have made little difference to the people of Loudville that their island was forgotten by the map makers. They still considered themselves as belonging to the town of Bristol, where they continued to vote and pay taxes. But when in the election of 1860 the result was changed in Bristol by throwing out the Loudville vote, the islanders were furious; and when during the Civil War they were called upon to supply more recruits for the town's quota under the draft laws than they thought fair, they rebelled. They cut their mainland ties, neither voting nor paying taxes, and for years successfully plowed their own political furrow. But today Maine's forgotten island is back in the Bristol fold.

Casco Bay is not so large as Penobscot Bay, as it does not indent the coast so deeply. The distance between Cape Elizabeth and Cape Small—marked in the center by Halfway Rock with its lighthouse —is over twenty miles, but the bay does not reach up into land more than fifteen miles. Its islands, however, outnumber those of any other bay. It is popularly said that they equal in number the days of the year, but this, of course, is an exaggeration. Actually there are 122 large, medium, and small islands, and this number could perhaps be stretched to 150 by counting the very smallest, the bare rocks where no man Friday could possibly leave a footprint. But there are quite enough without including these.

The islands fall naturally into three ranges—the outer, middle, and inner ranges—and there is scarcely an island without some interesting bit of legend or history attached to it: stories of smugglers, wreckers, pirates, Indians, witches, and early settlers. The very names of the islands are interesting: Junk of Pork, Pound of Tea, Stepping Stones, Bold Dick, Littlejohn, Rogue, Ministerial, White Bull, Brown Cow, Crow, Goose Nest, Whaleboat, Stave, Clapboard, Burnt Coat, etc. It is the most notable collection of islands on the Maine coast.

South of Cape Elizabeth the islands are not nu-

merous until you reach the cluster known as the
Isles of Shoals. But before you come to this group
there are one or two worth noticing. Richmond's
Island half a mile off the ancient town of Scarborough was orginally christened Isle of Bacchus
by Champlain, who found grapes growing there
which he thought were as good as those of his native country and if properly cultivated, would
make excellent wine. The island, which is about
three miles in circumference, does have good soil,
but nothing ever came of Champlain's suggestion.
Nor did the pagan name he gave the place stick.

The first settler seems to have been an Indian
trader named Richard Bagnall, generally called
Great Watt, who is thought to have established
himself on the island as early as 1628. But he did
not last long. Apparently he was an unprincipled
knave who cheated and robbed the Indians out-
rageously. Anyway, in 1631 the Indians crossed
over to the island and after killing Great Watt and
another man, looted and burned the trading house.

The following year John Winter, the agent of
Robert Trelawney, a merchant of Plymouth, England, visited the island with a view to establishing
a fishing station similar to the one at Monhegan.
Trelawney had been granted a patent of Cape
Elizabeth, including Richmond's Island. In the
spring of 1633, Winter returned with a crew of
men and the station was built. Winter brought his

family over from England, and the settlement flourished until broken up by his death.

The Winters had their troubles while on the island. In 1639 Trelawney received reports that Mrs. Winter was wont to beat her servant girl, Priscilla Beckford. He wrote to Winter, who replied as follows: "You write of some yll reports is given of my Wyfe for beatinge the maide: yf a faire waye will not doe yt, beatinge must sometimes vppon such Idlle girrels as she is. Yf you think yt fitte for my Wyfe to do all the work, and the maide sitt still, and she must forbear her hands to strike, then the work will ly vendonn. She hath bin now 2½ yeares in the house & I do not thinke she hath risen 20 tymes before my Wyfe hath bin vp to Call her, and many tymes light the fire before she comes out of her bed. She hath twice gone a mechinge in the woodes which we have bin fain to send all our Company to seek her. We can hardly keep her within doors after we are gonn to bed except we carry the kay of the door to bed with vs. She coulde never milke Cow nor Goate since she came hither. Our men do not desire to have her boyl the kittle for them she is so sluttish. She cannot be trusted to serve a few piggs but my Wyfe must commonly be with her. She hath written home I heare that she was fain to ly vppon goates skinns. She might take some goates skinns to ly in her bedd but not given to her for her lodginge. For a yeare & quarter or

more she lay with my daughter vppon a good
feather bed; before my daughter being lacke 3 or
4 days to Sacco the maid goes into bed with her
cloths & stockings & would not take the paines to
pluck off her Cloths; her bed after was a doust bedd
& shee had 2 Coverletts to ly on her, but Sheets she
had none, after that tyme she was found to be so
sluttish. Her beatinge that she hath had hath never
hurt her body nor limes. She is so fatt & soggy she
can hardly do any worke. Yf this maide at her
lazy tymes when she hath bin found in her yll ac-
cyons do not deserve 2 or 3 blowes I pray you who
hath the most reason to complain my Wyfe or
maide. My Wyfe hath an Vnthankefull office. Yt
does not please me well, being she hath taken so
much paines and care to order things as well as she
could, and ryse in the morning rath & go to bed soe
latte, and have hard speeches for yt."

If Mistress Winter had difficulty with the help in
the house, her husband fared no better outside with
his menservants and workmen, who were, he com-
plained, neither "plyable" nor "condishionable"
and "spoke Fair to the Face and Colloged behind
the back." His servants were wasters and pleasure
lovers and worked only when they pleased. Of one
of the workers he said, "He is such a talking Fellow
as makes our company worse than would be." If
any of these drones and trouble makers returned
to England, Winter thought they should be pun-

ished. Although Richmond's was no island Utopia, it was known as a well-managed plantation.

Boon Island, the lonely rock six miles southeastward of Cape Neddick, which extends out about a mile from York Beach, is Maine's cannibal island. In December, 1710, a vessel called the *Nottingham* was wrecked there, and the members of the crew who managed to get ashore on the island resorted to cannibalism to save their lives. They were on the rock for twenty-six days without any food or shelter worth mentioning, and it was only by rationing the body of the ship's carpenter who had died that they were able to hold out until rescued.

While such cases are rare, they are by no means unknown, even in modern times. Very harrowing was the experience of Erastus Cousins of Brooksville, Maine, who had a narrow escape from being eaten by his shipmates when the schooner *Augusta M. Gott* capsized in the Gulf Stream in 1868. The vessel while on her maiden voyage encountered a tropical hurricane which knocked her on her beam-ends. The crew of six men, all from Brooksville, were on the wreck for twelve days without anything to eat or drink. As a last desperate measure, it was decided to sacrifice one of their number and Cousins was chosen by lot to be the victim. His hungry mates were just about to butcher him when a sail was sighted. The ordeal left its mark on Erastus, who developed a stammer which remained with him forever. He did not go to sea again.

Although Boon Island has had a lighthouse since 1811, it is still occasionally the scene of a shipwreck. The last one was in February, 1944, when a 7,244-ton British freighter was split asunder by mountainous waves that lashed her for eighteen hours after she struck on Boon Island ledge in a raging North Atlantic storm. Twenty-five of her crew of forty-five were lost. The ship, which was carrying a general cargo, struck the ledge about two-thirty one Friday afternoon during a blinding snowstorm. At six a wireless message was sent from the ship saying she could not last much longer. At seven-thirty the order to abandon ship was given.

Chief Engineer Svend Haagensen said that all efforts to free the vessel failed. Mountainous seas broke over the ship all Friday afternoon and throughout the night. About eight-thirty Saturday morning she broke up with the bow still aground on the reef. After the breakup the forward section drifted off to the northward, then drifted back and grounded again. Apparently the stern section, which also drifted away, sank. Thirteen of the survivors were landed at Portland, seven at Portsmouth. They said the sea was strewn with wreckage for miles around. Of the twenty-five members of the crew who perished, the bodies of some were recovered.

The Isles of Shoals, lying five or six miles out in

the sea southeastward of the entrance to Portsmouth Harbor, belong partly to Maine and partly to New Hampshire. There are seven islands in the group, strung out for a distance of three miles in a general northeast and southwest direction. The four northernmost belong to Maine. Approaching from the north, the first one in the group is Duck Island, which is low and rocky and surrounded by dangerous ledges. A mile to the southwest is Appledore Island, formerly called Hog Island. It contains about 350 acres and is the largest of the group. A narrow channel separates it on the south from Smuttynose Island, sometimes referred to as Haley's Island. Smuttynose has about a hundred acres. On its south side it is connected by a breakwater with Cedar Island, the smallest of the group. Extending westward from Cedar Island is another breakwater connecting Cedar with Star Island. Star belongs to New Hampshire. It is about a hundred and fifty acres in extent, with a hotel on its northern side, a number of houses, and a steamboat landing. Half a mile to the westward of Star Island is Lunging Island, formerly known as Londoner's, a barren, rocky islet, with ledges on all sides. The southernmost of the group is White Island on which stands Isles of Shoals lighthouse.

For a century before the Revolution the islands were quite populous, containing at one time six hundred inhabitants, all engaged in fishing. But the war largely destroyed the commerce of the islands, and many people moved away and did not return. As late as the middle of the nineteenth century the best cod in the world came from the islands. They were sold in the market under the name Isles of Shoals dun fish. Between three and four thousand quintals were caught and cured each season. Although the island fish was highly esteemed, the islanders themselves were considered the rudest and most uncivilized beings in New England, with the exception of the Indians. At Newburyport, where they supplied the markets with fish, they were called Algerines.

From the period of the Revolution down to 1820 the Shoalers became terribly bestialized and degraded. Town meetings and all semblance of government organization were abandoned. As no records were kept, some of the inhabitants lost track of their ages. In a drunken orgy the meetinghouse was pulled down and burned. People mated without benefit of clergy, and the laws of consanguinity were ignored. The Reverend Jedediah Morse, who went to the islands in 1800, when the population was not much more than a hundred, made this note on the record of two marriages which he solemnized.

"The two couples above mentioned had been published eight or ten years (but not married), and cohabitated together since, and had each a

number of children. ———had been formerly
married to another woman; she had left him, and
cohabited with her uncle, by whom she has a number of children. No regular divorce had been obtained. Considering the peculiar deranged state of
the people on these islands, and the ignorance of
the parties, it was thought expedient, in order as
far as possible to prevent future sin, to marry
them."

Despite or perhaps because of the evil reputation
which clung to the place even after social conditions had been improved, people were attracted to
these desolate islands. This interest increased when
Thomas B. Laighton, the father of Cecelia Thaxter,
the poet, built a hotel on Appledore. Laighton was
a frustrated politician who wanted to escape from
the world and took for his hermitage the lighthouse on White Island. He was keeper of this lonely
beacon for a number of years, but finally moved
to Appledore, which was then uninhabited. Here
he built a house, where people began to drop in on
him, and from taking a few paying guests the ex-
hermit became a full-fledged landlord with a hotel
of his own. Hawthorne, Lowell, Thoreau, Whittier,
and many other notables came. As a result of the
publicity which his literary clientele gave the
islands, the place developed into a summer resort.

"It is quite impossible to give an idea of these
rocky shores," wrote Hawthorne, who was a guest

at Laighton's Hotel in the summer of 1852, "how confusedly they are tossed together, lying in all directions; what solid ledges, what great fragments thrown out from the rest. Often the rocks are broken, square and angular, so as to form a kind of staircase; though, for the most part, such as would require a giant stride to ascend them."

Mr. Laighton introduced Hawthorne to Mr. Thaxter, his son-in-law, and the two seem to have gotten on very well together. Hawthorne drank apple toddy at Thaxter's house, and Mrs. Thaxter, then a girl of eighteen, sang Negro melodies and other songs. Hawthorne said the toddy was "a very rich and spicy drink," and Cecelia Thaxter "sang like a bird."

Thaxter rowed Hawthorne to White Island, where they called at the lighthouse formerly kept by Mr. Laighton. The keeper had been a writing master, and, according to Hawthorne, had "a very sneaking kind of look." On the way back they landed at Londoner's Island. Here they flushed a brown owl from the rocks, which brought from Thaxter the information that white owls wintered at the Shoals, feeding on the rats that lived among the rocks. The rats originally came from vessels. Later, Mr. Laighton told Hawthorne that the artist who decorated Trinity Church in New York with sculpture wanted some real wings for a model for the wings of cherubim. Thaxter took him the wings of a white owl, and the sculptor gave his cherubim the wings of an owl.

Before Laighton built on Appledore none of the Shoalers would step foot on the island after dark, because they believed it was haunted. The ghost that prowled around the island was called Old Bab, and there were some people who claimed they had seen him. The story goes that Old Bab, who lived at the Shoals, had some connection with Captain Kidd. The pirate had come to the islands to bury his treasure, and as Old Bab knew where it had been hidden, he had been murdered for its protection. The legend has been the cause of much optimistic digging, particularly by men from Portsmouth. Apparently when Laighton built his hotel on Appledore he laid the ghost of Old Bab.

A grim story is told of a place on Star Island called Betty Moody's Hole. One of the features of the Isles of Shoals is the fissures and chasms in the rocks which are said to have appeared at the time of the Crucifixion, though how this could be known is a mystery. Betty Moody's Hole was formed by some great pieces of rock which covered over one of these fissures. It was here that she hid with her two children when the Indians landed on the island during King Philip's War. The Indians knew the men were away fishing and were bent on carrying off the women. Betty's children became frightened and began to cry. Fearful lest this should lead to their discovery, the distracted mother murdered the two children.

There was a memorable murder on Smuttynose Island the night of March 5, 1873, when Lewis Wagner, a German, who had worked at the Shoals as a fisherman, rowed out to the island from Portsmouth and in cold blood killed two Norwegian women, Anethe and Karen Christiansen, with an ax. Edmund Pearson told the story of the crime in his book, *Murder at Smuttynose*, published in 1926; but an even more remarkable account of it was written by Cecelia Thaxter in 1875. She was living at the Shoals at the time, and knew the people involved. Her account may be unique in American crime literature, for here was a trained author writing about a case of which she had direct knowledge.

If the islands of the New England coast were to be divided into those of the blessed and those of the damned, one would say without much hesitation that the Isles of Shoals belonged to the latter class.

Hawthorne was fascinated by the dark enchantment of the coastal islands of Maine and felt strongly the lure to possess one. He liked best the medium-sized island, with a portion of forest and a portion of cleared land. "The owner of such an island," he said, "must have a peculiar sense of proprietorship and lordship; he must feel more like his own master than other people can."

TO BE SUPERSTITIOUS

SUPERSTITION always strikes deep roots near the sea, and it is doubtful if it ever will become extinct, though it may go underground. It is too much a part of the racial inheritance of those whose forebears have for generations been closely associated with ships and the sea. Yet the dwellers along New England shores are probably no more superstitious than those who live away from the water. People everywhere seem to have their pet superstitions, though some are reluctant to own up to the fact.

Superstition was largely responsible for the breaking up of one of the early Maine settlements. General Samuel Waldo, the Boston merchant, who in pre-Revolutionary days owned the Muscongus Patent, which gave him an enormous tract of land in Maine, persuaded a considerable number of people living near Sterling in Scotland to emigrate to this country. A town was laid out for them on Broad Bay in Bristol, Maine. On a street half a mile long each settler was given a half-acre lot on which to build a log house. The place was named Sterling. Pioneering usually involved some hardships, and from the first the Scotch immigrants at Sterling met with many discouragements and disappointments, and were, moreover, assailed by strange sights and sounds. "Fireflies glowed in the dark woods. Frogs croaked in every swale, and loons screamed in the evening twilight." Against the wild New England background all the superstitions which these folk had brought from the fatherland were magnified tenfold. Contending with hunger and cold was bad enough, but fighting off witches and warlocks worse, and at length, their fears getting the better of them, they abandoned Sterling to the phantoms and it became a ghost town.

Although cases constantly arise to refute some

of the most popular superstitions, people persist in clinging to their beliefs. No superstition perhaps is better known or more implicitly believed than the one which holds that if anything goes wrong at the launching of a vessel misfortune will pursue her. The classic example of a ship that got off to a bad start but proved extremely lucky was the U.S. frigate *Constitution*, which is still alive and enjoying a quiet old age at the Charlestown Navy Yard. When the bark *Charles A. Littlefield*, which was built at Brewer in 1864, was launched, she shot across the river and ruined a wharf in Bangor, but she was never an unlucky vessel. This was the craft in which Lincoln Colcord, the author, was born off Cape Horn in 1883, while the vessel was under command of his father.

In one of the Boothbay cemeteries is a monument to the folly of acceding to superstition instead of defying it. It is a memorial to the thirteen Boothbay men who lost their lives when their vessel, the *C. G. Mathews*, a "banker," was wrecked at Prince Edward Island in the gale of October, 1851. The monument, which is an eight-foot shaft with an urn on top, has on its face a dramatic sketch of the doomed vessel, a two-master, driving on a rocky shore in a fearful storm. The curious feature of the catastrophe was that the lost crew had originally planned to go to the Grand Banks in the *G. W. Reed*, a new vessel which had just been launched. But at the launching there was a crowd of people on board, who followed the old custom of rolling the new vessel by rushing together from side to side. The unusual number of persons engaged in rocking her caused the *Reed* to roll over, rolling the rollers into the water. The incident was superstitiously taken to have a sinister significance, and the original crew refused to go in her, but went instead in the *C. G. Mathews.* Ironically enough, the *Reed* was in the same storm that wrecked the *Mathews,* but weathered it.

The belief is widely held that it is unlucky to begin a voyage on Friday, and those who hold to this view can cite the case of the *Herbert Fuller,* whose skipper had the temerity to sail on that day and was murdered on the high seas. Nor was he the only one to die on the voyage. His wife was also killed, and so was the second mate. The murder weapon used in this triple tragedy was an ax.

The *Herbert Fuller,* which was built at Harrington, Maine, in 1890, was a barkentine, meaning that she was a three-master, with the foremast square-rigged, the other two fore-and-aft rigged. During her first years she sailed from the near-by port of Machias, and most of her life she seems to have been engaged in the lumber-carrying trade.

One Friday in the summer of 1896 she sailed from Boston for Rosario, Argentina, with a cargo of lumber. She was commanded by Captain Charles

I. Nash of Harrington, who had a substantial interest in the vessel, and his wife also owned some shares in her. Mrs. Nash usually sailed with her husband, who had been a sea captain for twenty years.

The first mate was Thomas Mead Chambers Bram, a native of Saint Kitts in the British West Indies, probably the only place in the world to be recognized on the map under its nickname. Bram in his youth had run away from home to follow the sea. One of his first berths was in a schooner hailing from Eastport. Save for an occasional odd job ashore, he had spent most of his time afloat, serving as mate in several other ships besides the *Fuller*. Eight years before the tragic voyage he had become a naturalized citizen of the United States.

The rest of the crew was a mixed grill of various nationalities—Swedish, Finnish, Dutch, German, and French. Strangely enough, the *Fuller* also carried a passenger, a Harvard student named Lester H. Monks, who had embarked for reasons of health and also because he was fond of sailing and was eager to learn what a long voyage was like.

The voyage did not begin well. Bad weather and fog delayed the ship for a week or so before she could get to sea. Members of the crew had contrived to bring some liquor aboard and there was drinking among the men. Before the *Fuller* had logged many miles there was a sharp exchange of words between Bram and the captain, and between Bram and the second mate. Bram showed unpleasant symptoms of religious fanaticism.

When the *Fuller* was about seven hundred and fifty miles from Boston, Lester Monks was awakened at two in the morning by a woman's scream. This was followed by a gurgling sound which seemingly came from the chart room where Captain Nash slept. Monks called the captain a couple of times, but received no answer. He then loaded his revolver and went to investigate. To his horror he found that the captain and his wife had been brutally murdered, apparently with an ax.

Monks then went to find the first mate. Bram was on deck. Monks told him what had happened and conducted him to the scene of the crime. Bram was afraid it was a case of mutiny, and the two remained on deck all night, Bram keeping watch over Charley Brown, the man at the wheel, while Monks kept a lookout forward for any move from that quarter.

It was not, however, a case of mutiny. The crew was shocked when at dawn they were told of the crime. Shortly afterwards the steward found the body of the second mate. He had been murdered in the same ghastly way as the others.

It was a terrifying situation for the survivors. All knew that the murderer was still on the ship, but his identity remained a mystery. By common consent the bloodstained ax which had been discovered was thrown overboard, lest the murderer take it into his head to use it on someone else.

Within a few days the condition of the dead bodies made it impossible to keep them on the ship any longer. Bram favored burial at sea, but he was overruled, and they were placed in one of the boats and towed astern on a long line. The *Fuller*, it was decided, should be taken into some convenient port, and accordingly she was headed for Halifax. Bram was emotionally upset by the whole affair and broke down and cried several times. Before the nightmare voyage was ended the crew put the mate and Charley Brown, who had been at the wheel the night of the murder, in irons.

Bram was indicted for the murders and was tried twice in the Federal Court at Boston. The first trial resulted in a verdict of guilty of murder in the first degree, and Bram was sentenced to be hanged. His lawyers, however, succeeded in getting him a new trial. He was convicted again at his second trial, but this time without capital punishment.

At both trials the defense charged that Charley Brown was the real murderer, and the case at one point seemed to turn on the question of whether or not Brown could have left the wheel long enough to kill three persons without the ship's falling off her course. Expert testimony was introduced on this point of seamanship, nine ancient mariners swearing that he could have lashed the wheel and left it for ten or twenty minutes. But at the second trial Captain Nash's brother, who had taken command of the *Fuller*, testified that her sails would flap in two minutes if the helm were lashed.

By the time Bram was sent to prison for the murders the Spanish-American War had broken out. He served some fifteen years in Atlanta, and in 1913 was paroled. At the expiration of the parole in 1919, President Wilson, while in Paris for the Peace Conference, granted him a full pardon.

The name of the *Herbert Fuller* was changed to the *Margaret B. Rouss*. She was in service for many years, but late in April, 1917, shortly after the United States entered World War I, she was torpedoed by a German U-boat in the Mediterranean. She was an unconscionable time dying because she was loaded with lumber, and finally a boarding party from the submarine blew her up with bombs. The crew in a lifeboat rowed forty-five miles to Monte Carlo, where they were befriended by the Prince of Monaco and James Gordon Bennett, the publisher, who arranged for their return home.

The Bram case attracted great attention because it was one of circumstantial evidence and no motive for the murders was established. People in Harrington believe that the motive was jealousy, but the usual explanation is that Bram did it as a result of some queer religious quirk. Others point to the fact that the *Herbert Fuller* sailed on Friday.

Strange to relate, another Harrington sea captain and his wife also lost their lives at sea. Templeton Fickett was captain of an iron four-master. The vessel came in with the captain and his wife missing. The explanation was that they had been washed overboard in a storm, but Harrington people always thought they had been murdered.

"He was a mild-mannered man," Captain Ralph J. Frye, a native of Harrington, who knew Fickett, explained to me, "but they say he was tough on shipboard."

The old sea superstition of the Flying Dutchman has its hybrid version in Maine. The captain of the Dutch ship, it will be recalled, cursed God and was condemned to sail the seas forever without putting into any port. This phantom ship has since been reported many times. Whittier based his famous poem, "The Dead Ship of Harpswell," on a fireside legend of a specter vessel seen at Orrs Island. The ship never came to port; when near the shore she always drifted out to sea again. This is not Maine's only ghost ship. In *An Account of Two Voyages to New England* (1674), John Josselyn speaks of a ship in a small cove on the coast of Maine, with a great red horse standing by the mainmast. He thought the ship was produced by witches. He says it "vanished of a suddain."

It used to be considered a bad thing to have clergymen, lawyers, or women on board sailing vessels. Why they should have been looked upon with disfavor is not clear. Perhaps in the case of the clergy it was because in the past their duties on shipboard included the consolation of the sick and the burial of the dead. A further reason may have been that since the reverend gentlemen were mortal enemies of the devil, seamen were afraid the Evil One might attempt the clergymen's destruction by doing some mischief to the ship. Lawyers were looked upon as a class of persons who were up to no good anyway, and it was just plain bad luck to have the rascals around. Nobody seems to know why there should have been any prejudice against women, except perhaps that they were a nuisance on shipboard. Originally the superstition about them may have been based on a fear of witches and their necromancy. In Maine it was customary for the wives of many sea captains to go voyaging with their husbands, and nothing was thought of it; but some people on the coast still believe it is bad luck to have a woman on board a fishing vessel.

Recently a fisherman's wife told a friend of mine that one day last spring a bird flew in where her husband had some seines stored and lighted on the nets. She said at once that it would bring bad luck. During the sardine season her husband had the good fortune to impound twenty thousand bushels of sardine herring in his seine. At the prevailing price his catch was worth $30,000. He was almost beside himself with elation, when suddenly the seine, which was under great pressure, parted before his eyes and the fish escaped into the deeper water offshore. The fisherman made a few other catches during the summer, but they were all small, and his net income for the season didn't amount to much.

A bird, however, may bring good luck to a vessel. The brig *Robin*, which was built at Winterport in 1857, was so named because while the vessel was under construction a pair of robins built a nest under the bow. Work was delayed and the launching held up until the young birds had left the nest. Lincoln Colcord states that the vessel was always extremely lucky.

Certainly in Maine it has never been thought unlucky to bestow the name of a bird on a vessel. There has been a flock of eagles—*Golden Eagle, National Eagle, Flying Eagle, War Eagle*, and just plain *Eagle*. Other vessels have borne such names as *Chanticleer, Lark, Dove, Nightingale, Cygnet, Osprey, Parrot, Raven, Hawk, Black Swan*, and *Albatross*. The *Nightingale* was a clipper named for Jenny Lind, the Swedish Nightingale. Even Audubon the bird man had a vessel named for him.

Cats, which are almost universally disliked by sailors, seem to have been regarded with a certain measure of tolerance in Maine, though I have been told that to have a cat leave a vessel is almost as bad as having the rats depart. The vessel will not return.

Some localities and even families have their own private superstitions, but everywhere you find people who deliberately defy all such notions, and no harm seems to befall them.

TO BUILD SHIPS AND SAIL
THE OCEAN WIDE

EXCEPT in wartime, the going down to the sea in ships has been robbed of most of its terrors and much of its romance. It is no longer a setting out upon a great and uncertain adventure. Almost all the fears the sea inspired have vanished. Its prestige has been largely lost. Only by recalling the days of sail can the glamour be recaptured.

There is no more exciting chapter in the maritime history of Maine than that which records the exploits of her men-of-war. One is most likely to remember her mercantile ships and to forget the privateers that swarmed out of her ports during the Revolution and the War of 1812. With the abolition of privateering, the term "man-of-war" has come to be restricted in its application to vessels belonging to the regularly organized navy of a country, but formerly it applied to any vessel whose chief purpose was fighting. Scores of vessels were built or fitted out for privateering, most of them small and armed with only a few guns or with nothing more formidable than muskets. They were built for speed and their success depended on this and also on the boldness and dash of the commanders and the seamanship and fighting qualities of the crews. It was admittedly waging war for profit, but there was nothing disreputable about it, and the activities of the privateers aided the country.

It was a risky business and many of them came to grief. Numerous privateersmen underwent the horrors of confinement in the British prison hulks or other places of detention. But some of the ships were enormously successful, bringing in rich prizes that paid handsome dividends to the backers and crews. They were usually built on shares and a large proportion of the population of the coast was involved directly or indirectly in privateering. A single cruise sometimes netted the owners several hundred thousand dollars. One captured cargo which proved something of a disappointment was found to consist mainly of Bibles.

Maine as a great shipbuilding headquarters turned out privateers not only for local adventurers but for outside interests as well. The famous privateer, *Grand Turk*, was Maine built and Salem owned. Constructed at Wiscasset in 1812, this brig was a noted fast sailer. For speed no vessels could equal the best American-built privateers. In this there was good reason for pride.

Commodore Edward Preble of Portland, the first great commander of the American Navy, began his career afloat at the age of sixteen by enlisting in a privateer. In 1777, while working on his father's farm, he threw down his hoe and with the declaration, "I am through with farming," went down to the harbor and joined a European-bound privateer from Newburyport on a cruise that lasted a year.

At the age of eighteen, as a midshipman in the Massachusetts State Marine, he boarded and captured a British brig in Penobscot Bay right under the enemy's guns and brought his prize safely away. Later he was himself captured and confined in the notorious prison ship *Jersey* in New York Harbor. He was paroled and eventually released, thanks to the kindly efforts of Colonel William Tyng, a prominent tory citizen of Portland, who had been a friend of young Preble's father, General Jedediah Preble.

After the war Preble continued to follow the sea in peaceful merchantmen until 1798, when he was commissioned a lieutenant in the United States Navy. He was given command of the new frigate *Essex,* in which he escorted a convoy of mercantile ships to the East Indies and became the first naval officer to carry the American flag around the Cape of Good Hope. But his greatest exploit was his victorious campaign against the Barbary pirates. His flagship in that expedition was the famous frigate *Constitution.* In 1803, off the coast of Spain on his way to Tripoli, a strange ship rushed up out of the night abeam of *Old Ironsides.* Preble stepped out on the quarter-deck.

"Give me the speaking trumpet, Mr. Robinson, and get the crew to quarters . . . . I now hail for the last time. If you do not answer, I'll fire a shot into you."

"If you do, I'll answer with a broadside."

"I should like to see you try that! I now hail for an answer. What ship is that?"

"This is His Britannic Majesty's 84-gun ship *Donegal,* Sir Richard Strachan. Send a boat at once."

"This is the U. S. frigate *Constitution,* 44, Captain Edward Preble, and I'll be damned if I send a boat aboard any ship. Blow your matches, boys, we're going to fight."

The English commodore had lied about the

strength and identity of his ship. One of the stranger's boats with a lieutenant soon came alongside the *Constitution*.

In 1806, after his return home, Commodore Preble received orders from the government to build nine war vessels for the Navy at Portland. Eight were to be gunboats, and the ninth a bomb ketch. Preble drew the plans for them, and on August 23, 1807, the new vessels sailed from Portland for New York. The squadron was under the command of Lieutenant James Lawrence who was killed in action during the War of 1812 while in command of the *Chesapeake*. His dying orders were, "Tell the men to fire faster and not to give up the ship; fight her till she sinks."

Two days after the ships had sailed, Commodore Preble died of consumption. He did much to establish the prestige of the young American Navy. Because many men who served with him and whom he helped to develop later became distinguished naval officers, Commodore Preble came to be known as the father of the United States Navy. Among the men were Stephen Decatur, Isaac Hull, and Oliver Hazard Perry.

Maine has always been an important source of ships in wartime. They have been building ships in Maine for three hundred years, and the necessary knowledge and skill have been handed down for generations. It is a traditional art that has never been lost. When war was declared in 1941, the Maine shipbuilders as usual went to work with a vengeance. Not only were destroyers and merchantmen produced, but great numbers of wooden vessels of all kinds, for minesweeping, for patrol and pursuit work, and for many other special needs of modern warfare. Steel was scarce and wooden ships were in demand.

There was, of course, enormous activity at the famous Bath Iron Works, where destroyers have been built for many years. Two large new yards were built at South Portland for the mass production of merchant vessels by the new method of building ships in basins. Thousands of workers had to be trained for this special work.

Meanwhile, thousands of others were already busy in scores of shipyards up and down the coast building wooden vessels ahead of schedule. Some of these yards were large, others quite small. One I remember employed only fifteen men, who ranged in age from fifteen to eighty-five. A friend of mine who worked in this yard had learned shipbuilding in his youth in a Rockland shipyard, where his father had been employed for many years before him. After the first World War when the shipbuilding industry suffered a slump he turned to carpentering. When that got bad during the depression he became a house painter and paper hanger. He was glad to get back to work at the traditional family trade.

"In the old shipbuilding days," he said, "there were many gangs of specialists—inboard joiners and outboard joiners, calkers and riggers, and so on—who went from shipyard to shipyard along the coast as their services were needed; but now when a man goes to work in the morning he doesn't know what kind of work he will be asked to do."

The old-time master builders liked to work from models. They preferred to take the lines of a vessel from a wooden half-model instead of from a blueprint. They could tell what kind of vessel she was to be and whether she would be a good sailer or not. It was easier than looking at a plan and trying to visualize in the mind what she was like.

Native oak is still generally used for the keels of the wooden ships built in Maine. It is the practice of many shipbuilders to soak the oak in fresh or salt water for several weeks before using it. After the keel has been laid and tipped up and the frame for the stern set, the ribs are swung into place. The framing has to be done perfectly or the vessel will not be true. There are legends of master builders who could fair up a ship with the naked eye, but usually it is done by actual and careful measurement.

After the framing comes the planking, which requires experience to be done properly. The old method was to peg the planks in place as snugly as possible with wooden trunnels. The holes were bored with augers and the tree nails driven in and wedged in, making an all-wood hull. A badly planked vessel was apt to spew her oakum when she got to sea and there was no telling what might happen then.

Eventually the time for launching arrives, when the keel blocks are knocked out and the ship slides down the greased ways to take the water with beauty. At least, it is hoped she will slide easily because, as stated elsewhere, it is considered bad luck to have a ship stick on the ways.

The tonnage figures given for old sailing vessels may sometimes be misleading because a different method of measurement was used. The old way was to multiply the length by three-quarters of the extreme width, and that result by the depth, and then divide the product by ninety-five. The result was about one-third greater than that reached by the present method.

It is not unusual to find tools and other appurtenances of shipbuilding and seafaring in old Maine houses—adzes and great augers for boring holes for trunnels; chains, charts, and compasses; sea chests and similar objects of a nautical character, to say nothing of the curiosities brought home from the four quarters of the globe.

In a typical story-and-a-half house with conch

shells beside the front door I found an old compass with a wooden bowl and the imprint of the Portland maker on the card. It also had on its face a Masonic emblem—a pair of compasses and a square at the due east point. It had collected dust in the attic for years, but it was easily cleaned and made shipshape.

From another old house came a stack of account books beautifully kept in the old brown ink that used to come in china bottles. The accounts covered the expenses of various schooners between the years 1845 and 1865, and included disbursements for such articles as a marling spike 50¢, stick for topgallant yard 75¢, a quadrant $7.50, a clam hoe 50¢, an accordion $1.50, a tin horn 50¢, and a spyglass $6.00. Other purchases were for ballast, water, wood, salt, hemp rope, blocks, oakum, spar varnish, and duck. There were entries of money paid for calking, for repairing sails and rigging, and for fixing compasses. Charges also appeared for pilotage, pierage or wharfage, skowage or scow hire, and ferriage. There was even a night-school tuition fee, "Navigation 8 evenings 88¢." The names of some of the schooners were the *Ocean Romp, Prima Donna, Silver Moon, Village Belle, Young Sultan, Caravan,* and *Eastern Queen.*

There was something in a name when it came to christening a vessel. A saucy name often helped to attract crews, while an odd or outlandish one sometimes had the opposite effect. Of the thousands of ships built along the Maine coast and up the rivers, by far the greater number were named for people. Vessels frequently bore the name of the owner, but more often that of his wife or children. Among popular feminine names given to some of the first vessels were *Susan, Sarah, Sally, Polly,* and *Nancy*.

Famous women were sometimes honored, among them Venus, Sappho, Pocahontas, and Martha Washington. There were no movie stars in those days, but Lola Montez and Jenny Lind had Maine vessels named for them, and presumably these ships had figureheads that were likenesses of the ladies. The schooner *Melissa Trask*, built at Brewer in 1880, had the reputation of being the homeliest vessel ever built in the Penobscot area.

Small children were sometimes remembered when a vessel was christened. *Little Cherub, Young James*, and *Little William* are obviously juvenile names.

National heroes came in for their share of nautical glory, including Daniel Boone, Kit Carson, and Daniel Webster. Many presidential names were used, which as a rule makes it easy to date the vessels. A schooner called the *Andrew Johnson* or the *Millard Fillmore* clearly belongs to a definite period. It is fairly plain that a vessel named *Tippecanoe* refers to General William Henry Harrison.

But to make certain I looked up the date of her building and found this to be true. She was launched in 1840, the year of the Hard Cider Campaign, when the Whigs of Maine surprised themselves by electing their candidate for governor, which was taken as an indication of the way the country would go in the November presidential election. The victory gave rise to the campaign song:

> Oh have you heard how old Maine went?
> She went hell-bent for Governor Kent,
> And Tippecanoe and Tyler, too.

Literature has also played a part in Maine's nautical nomenclature, with vessels named *Shakespeare, Don Quixote, Sancho Panza, John Bunyan, Don Juan,* and the *Wandering Jew.*

But there is no use in pursuing the matter any farther. The shipping lists are fathoms long.

QUARRYING, which is a very ancient industry, has been carried on in Maine since colonial days. Limestone has been excavated in the Penobscot Bay region for more than two centuries, and granite for over a hundred years. Slate has likewise been quarried in Maine for the best part of a century, though not on the same scale as limestone and granite.

The first limestone quarry was opened at

Thomaston in 1733 on the hill where the state prison now stands. Near by, William McIntyre had a kiln in which he burned lime for the Boston market. Brigadier General Samuel Waldo, who was interested in the development of this region, also engaged in the lime trade, sending his vessels up the Saint George's River to Thomaston for cargoes of the burned form of the quarried rock. General Henry Knox, the Boston bookseller, who married Brigadier Waldo's great-granddaughter and was our first Secretary of War, settled at Thomaston in 1795, where lime and lumber were among his chief interests. Others entered the business which grew apace, until the countryside from Thomaston to Camden was gashed with quarries. Kilns multiplied and a century after the first one was built, stone was being burned into lime on the western side of Penobscot Bay at the rate of 750,000 casks a year.

Rockland, which was originally part of Thomaston, became the center of the lime business. In 1858 twelve limestone quarries were in operation there. The gray face of the rock was blasted with explosives and quarried with hammer, pick, and shovel. The stone was then carried in oxcarts down to the kilns beside the harbor. It required 125 of the old-style wood-burning kilns to reduce the rock to lime, of which about 900,000 casks were produced, a figure exceeded later. It took a fleet of three hundred vessels to carry this lime to market, while several hundred more were kept busy fetching wood to feed the furnaces. Rockland harbor was crowded with shipping and the air smelled of wood smoke.

A kiln consumed thirty cords of wood for each burning of rock, and the kiln-wooders, as the small vessels which brought the fuel were called, converged on Rockland from every nook and corner of the coast. They even came from the maritime provinces. The Saint John wood-boats were famous for their odd appearance and cheap construction. Because of the buoyant character of their cargoes they were crudely built and were anything but trim and seaworthy in appearance. It was said that they made as much money selling liquor as wood. But the American boats were about as bad. They were poorly made and just as unlovely. They were broad beamed and square sterned. Few sported bowsprits. They carried a single sail on a mast stepped far forward to make room for as large a deckload of cordwood as possible. This load was usually so high that the man at the wheel could not see to steer and was guided by shouted instructions from a lookout on the woodpile. When the lime kilns went over to coal and later to oil, this gallimaufry of strange craft vanished like plum blossoms in a gale.

Very different were the Rockland limers, the

coasters which delivered the casks of lime along the seaboard. They had to be well constructed, because lime is a dangerous cargo. If it gets wet it starts to burn, defying all the usual methods of fire fighting. To load a leaky vessel with lime was to invite disaster. If the lime became slaked, it began to smoulder and the only way to save the vessel was to try to smother the fire by sealing the hatches and keeping all air from reaching the cargo. The vessel then made the nearest port, anchoring well away from other shipping, where the outcome was anxiously awaited. Weeks sometimes passed before the captain and crew knew. Meanwhile, the vessel was liable to go up in flames at any moment. Lime is still manufactured at Rockland, but steel barges and tugs have replaced the old limers and reduced the fire hazard.

Not much granite quarrying was done in Maine prior to 1830, but before the end of the nineteenth century it had grown into a great industry. Fortunately the best belts of granite were to be found in southern Maine close to tidewater. Granite is heavy stuff to handle, and the cost of transporting it has always been one of the industry's major problems. But the easy accessibility of the principal Maine quarries, situated on the seaward peninsulas, the coastal islands, and the banks of navigable rivers, gave the business the economic advantage of cheap transportation. By 1890, when

loads of granite were being used in building, Maine
led all states in its production, and the bulk of it
was shipped in vessels directly from the quarries.

Cheap transportation, however, was not solely
responsible for Maine's taking the lead. Maine
granite comes in a variety of colors, grains, and
textures, which make it suitable for many different
purposes, and it has been used in the construction
of many noted buildings, bridges, and monuments
in different parts of the country.

The colors range from light gray to black—depending on whether the dominant minerals are
black or white and are strongly or weakly con-
trasted—and from dark red to light pink, buff, and
pale lavender. Some of the gray and black granites
have a greenish tinge. The dark-red granite is
found at Head Harbor Island and Hardwood Island
on Moosabec Reach. There are a dozen quarries of
black granite, three of them on tidewater, one at
Round Pond on Muscongus Bay, another at Vinalhaven in Penobscot Bay, and still another at Addi-
son on Pleasant River, a few miles above Pleasant
Bay. This granite, which is used only for costly
work, takes a beautiful polish, and the contrast between the hammered surface and the polished surface is very striking indeed. For one reason or
another, often because of the color, the granite of
a particular quarry may be in special request.

Apart from the color, the use to which granite

can be put depends on the way it splits. As in the case of almost every kind of stone, there are joints or planes along which it parts easily, and it is the position of these rifts, their placement close together or far apart, that is the deciding factor. In some quarries the parting planes are so near one another that the granite can be used only for paving blocks, curbing, sills, and similar small productions. At other quarries the parting planes are so far apart that stone of almost any size can be quarried. It was at the old Palmer quarry on Vinalhaven Island that eight huge monoliths were turned out for the Cathedral of St. John the Divine in New York. These columns were over fifty feet long and six feet thick. They were turned on a giant granite lathe capable of taking a column seventy feet by seven. The first column broke after it was removed from the lathe, so the others were turned in two sections.

Texture, too, is important in appraising the commercial possibilities of granitic rocks. Coarse-textured granite is perhaps best for massive structures, while the fine-textured is better for lighter structures, monuments, and statues. Some coarse-grained rock may be all right for rough building material, but unfit for dressed building stone. For coarse carving in the higher parts of buildings coarse-textured stone may perhaps be used, but in such granites large feldspars crossing the sculptured design at various angles are apt to produce lines and reflections at odds with the lights and shades produced by the sculptor's design and thus spoil the effect. Medium-grained, even-textured granite, uniform in color, and largely free from dark segregations or knots, and from pyrites and other minerals that may cause stains on exposure, is probably the best for all-round use.

In the days when cities paved their streets with granite, the Maine coast quarries supplied one-seventh of the paving blocks used in the United States. Paving stones were a by-product of many quarries; material which otherwise would have gone to waste was used—thin sheets of granite and stone disfigured by knots and sap. It was not unusual for a quarry where the men were engaged chiefly in cutting and dressing construction stone to produce 100,000 paving blocks a year as a side line.

There were many quarries, however, that turned out nothing but paving stones. Most of the quarries on Spruce Head Island were dedicated to this branch of the industry, and some three hundred men were employed in the work. A quarryman could knock out two hundred or more paving stones a day, for which he was paid five cents apiece. Most of the drilling here was done by hand, so no expensive equipment was required to deal with the product. The openings from which the granite was taken were often quite small, and were called motions. Spruce Head was not then a bridged island, so the men had to be ferried across the narrow stretch of water separating it from the mainland. It cost them five cents apiece each way.

Different cities used paving stones of different sizes. New York, where a good deal of Maine granite pavement remains, favored blocks eleven to fourteen inches long, four inches wide, and seven inches thick. Over these stones rolled the ironbound wheels of the commercial traffic of other years, the hoofs of the horses making the sparks fly as they brought their great roughshod feet down forcefully on the granite blocks. Over these same stones heavy motor trucks rumble today.

Paving stones were shipped in coastwise schooners, the vessels at some places, as at Minturn on Swan's Island, coming right alongside the quarry to load. The stones were sluiced into the holds. They were run against bumpers which wore out rapidly under the bombardment.

A granite cargo, whether in large or small blocks, was hard on a vessel, and often it was only when a coaster became superannuated and unfit even for the lumber trade that it took to carrying granite cargoes. Old and gray, with patched and dingy sails, some of them looked like vagabonds of the sea. A number of these old-timers, deep-laden with granite, were lost.

The smaller coasters could carry about a hundred and fifty tons of granite; the larger ones, like the *Nancy Hanks,* a four-master, which was for some time in the service of the Deer Island Granite Company at its Crotch Island quarry, could carry seven or eight hundred tons. The *Nancy Hanks* would leave with granite and return with coal. This company now uses seagoing barges and tugs; it takes a tow about a week to reach New York from Deer Isle. A derrick boat is used to take granite to Searsport for shipment by rail. Crotch Island lies just across Deer Island Thoroughfare from Stonington on Deer Isle, and the quarry workers are ferried across the thoroughfare in one of the old boats of the Maine Seacoast Mission.

It is only the men who work at the face of the rock who are called quarrymen. Then there are the cutters, the sawyers, the carvers, the polishers, and others with special jobs down to the dynamite boy. The carvers are the highest paid. They are the artists in stone who execute the sculptural designs and decorations, working from plaster models. Carvers have to serve a four years' apprenticeship.

Although granite has been quarried in Maine all the way from York to Calais, there is not so much activity now as there was before artificial stone and concrete became popular as building materials. Still, considerable granite continues to be quarried. Bridge stone and granite veneering for buildings are in demand, some paving material is produced, and there are calls for granite for other miscellaneous uses. The Maine quarries have always been an important source of mausoleum stone. The tombs of General Grant and George Gershwin were both built of Maine granite.

Like the limestone business, granite quarrying has been largely centered around Penobscot Bay. The limestone quarries are on the mainland, the granite workings mostly on the islands. The granite quarries are of no great depth, not averaging more than thirty feet, though some which cover from five to eight acres are among the most extensive in the United States. Some of the limestone quarries are over two hundred feet deep.

At least one granite island in the bay has become a ghost town. Hurricane Island, which lies a little more than two miles southwest of Vinalhaven, was once a town in its own right, with a church, a school, and numerous homes, but today it is deserted. General Tillson, who owned the island, began granite quarrying there in 1870, but the real development began in 1878, when the Booth brothers of New York took over the island for quarrying operations and built a town for their workers on the hillside overlooking Hurricane Sound. It had been a part of Vinalhaven, but that year it was set off and incorporated. The town was noted for its small size, its superb granite, and the fact **that** the state dry law was actually enforced there.

Hurricane Island prospered for some time. When the quarry was going full blast, between three and four hundred men were employed. Hurricane is in the important belt of granite that extends southwestward from Brooklin on the eastern side of the bay to Vinalhaven, taking in Deer Isle and the neighboring islands on the way. The granite is gray to pinkish gray in color and in grain ranges from fine to coarse. It is mostly the medium-textured pink granite that is quarried. At Hurricane it could be easily wrought, as it lay near the surface and split in horizontal sheets. It is said that one of these sheets blasted in the quarry measured five hundred feet long, twenty feet wide, and nearly forty feet in depth. That blast must have shaken the island worse than any hurricane. Granite from the quarry was used in many public buildings that are still standing, but there is nothing much left at Hurricane Island now except a few rusty boilers and derelict derricks.

Slate quarrying in Maine has been confined chiefly to two towns in the central part of the state, Brownville and Monson in Piscataquis County. A belt of clay slate sweeps across the state of Maine in a southwesterly direction from near the eastern boundary to the Kennebec, passing to the southward of Mt. Katahdin and Moosehead Lake. It is in this belt that the two towns are situated.

The first slate quarry seems to have been that of the Bangor and Piscataquis Slate Company opened at Brownville in 1843, which sent out from eight to ten thousand squares of slate annually. In 1846 the Merrill quarry was opened. Mr. Merrill bought fifteen hundred acres of land along the slate ridge and erected buildings requiring thirty thousand squares of roofing. Later came the Highland quarry. Welshmen were imported to work the slate, and at the Centennial Exposition at Philadelphia in 1876 Brownville slate won first place as the finest roofing slate in the land. But only Welsh names and heaps of broken slate near the pits remain to remind one of the vanished quarry business. Monson developed later as a quarry center and has lasted longer. The quality of its slate is unbeatable.

F<small>IS</small>H and potatoes have long been leading items on Maine's bill of fare. Two lines of homespun verse, current for generations along the coast, show how highly these articles of food were regarded, and no nonsense about the matter, either.

Fish and potatoes, the fat of the land;
If you won't eat that, you can starve and be
damned.

There was a time, however, when the potato had no social standing and was almost completely ignored. It bore, in fact, a rather evil reputation, and for the first century of the colonial period was rarely planted in New England. For one thing, it wasn't mentioned in the Bible. Then the suspicion intruded that it was the forbidden fruit of the Garden of Eden. From this it was an easy step to the belief that it was a powerful aphrodisiac. This notion nearly got one minister into trouble with his church. The wicked fellow actually raised twenty bushels of the exciting things. By a last absurdity, there were people as late as the time of the Stamp Act who believed that a daily diet of spuds would terminate a person's life in seven years. But gradually the poor potato made its way, its virtues slowly overcoming all hostility, until it appeared on the menu of the commencement dinners at Harvard.

It is traditionally believed that the first New Englanders to begin the regular cultivation of the potato were the Scotch-Irish pioneers who settled at Londonderry, New Hampshire, in 1719. From there it spread throughout New England, soon taking root in Maine, where it prospered better than anywhere else. The climate and soil were admirably suited to its cultivation. This was notably the case in the vast Aroostook region in northeastern Maine, which is today the greatest potato producing section of the United States.

The first settlements in this area, which is larger
than the state of Connecticut, were established
along the Saint John River by Acadian French refu-
gees who fled from the Minas Basin in Nova Scotia
in the eighteenth century to escape transportation
and separation by the English authorities in America. These exiles from the Evangeline country, men,
women, and children, followed the course of the
Saint John in their bateaux, until they came to a
Malecite Indian village in the primeval forest bordering the stream. The French knew how to get
along amicably with the Indians, and with their
consent landed at what is now the village of Saint
David, where today a large white cross behind the
church marks the first Acadian landing place, while
across the river on the Canadian side is the Malecite Indian reservation. Other settlements followed
along the Saint John, where it forms the extreme
northeast boundary line. Many villages in this sec-
tor are still wholly or predominantly inhabited by
French-speaking descendants of the Acadians. They
live mostly a pastoral life in which the potato plays
an important part.

Although these Acadian settlements were the
first in Aroostook County, they were not the most
important. The movement which led to the greatest development of the country began when American pioneers commenced to drift into the region
around Houlton, during the early decades of the

nineteenth century. Only a few came in the beginning because it was a long and perilous journey through the wilderness, and once the place was reached there was nothing much to do but chop down trees. Lumbering was for years the chief industry, but owing to the remoteness and isolation of the region even this was attended with difficulties.

It was the historical side show known as the Aroostook War that focused attention on this immense stretch of moose and caribou country. By the treaty of 1782, the Saint Croix River had been agreed upon as the dividing line between the United States and Canada, but strange to say, there was a dispute as to which of three rivers emptying into Passamaquoddy Bay was the true Saint Croix. In 1796 commissioners appointed by the two governments settled the question, but beyond the monument marking the head of the river the line was not definitely fixed. It was wild land and there was no pressing need for an immediate settlement. But following the War of 1812 a joint commission, including English and American engineers, undertook to run the line, which was to continue northward from the Saint Croix until the highlands dividing the streams flowing into the Saint Lawrence and those flowing toward the Atlantic were reached.

All ran smoothly until they came to Mars Hill, a

lonely and segregated mountain thirty miles north of Houlton and a few miles west of the Saint John River. This landmark is a long elevation trending north and south with a peak at each end. Trees were felled and a place cleared on both peaks. It was then ascertained that the northern peak was 1370 feet and the southern one 1519 feet above the tidal waters of the Saint Lawrence. The English engineers immediately claimed that the highlands had been reached, which the Americans denied, saying that the highlands were far to the north. The dispute waxed warm and resulted in the party's breaking up, each side leaving to report to its government.

In 1828 the United States as a precautionary measure sent seven companies of infantry to Houlton, where a frontier post was established on Garrison Hill, with barracks, officers' quarters, and other buildings, none of which survive today, though the site is worth visiting for the view from the old parade ground. The federal government also authorized the building of a military road through the wilderness from Bangor to Houlton, a distance of 120 miles. This proved a boom to the pioneers already in the border country and opened up the Aroostook area to new settlers. Although often clogged with snow in winter and impassable in the spring, it was the first direct route to the region.

Both the United States and Great Britain claimed

the French settlements along the Saint John near the mouth of the Madawaska River. In June, 1837, an American government agent, while taking a census of these settlements, was arrested by a Canadian civil officer on a charge of exciting the people to sedition and was taken to Fredericton, New Brunswick. It was a trumped-up charge intended by the British as notice to Maine that it would no longer be allowed to exercise any jurisdiction over the disputed territory. Governor Dunlap of Maine promptly declared that Maine had been invaded by a foreign power and ordered the militia to be ready for military duty. But as the agent was soon released and there were no further incidents, the excitement died down.

Trouble flared up again in 1839, when a Maine land agent reported that Canadian lumbermen from New Brunswick were in the debatable territory, stealing the best timber around the Aroostook River. A sheriff with a posse of two hundred men was sent to expel the trespassers, who retreated into New Brunswick but stood their ground at Woodstock, after breaking into the government arsenal and arming themselves. The Maine land agent was taken prisoner, but the sheriff, seeing that there would be serious bloodshed, possibly leading to war, if the posse and the lumberers clashed, wisely withdrew. He had hardly had time to lay the matter before the governor at Augusta when the proclamation of Governor Harvey of New Brunswick arrived, declaring that British territory had been invaded and that he intended to meet it with force.

The back-fence controversy now took a serious turn. Maine's answer was the appropriation of eight hundred thousand dollars for the defense of the public lands, and the governor ordered out ten thousand militia. When the news reached Washington, Congress backed up Maine by appropriating ten million dollars and authorizing the president to raise fifty thousand volunteers for six months, if Governor Harvey of New Brunswick endeavored to carry out his intention of exercising exclusive authority over the boundary lands.

Early in March, General Winfield Scott and his staff reached Augusta. He got in touch with Governor Harvey, and the situation was soon saved by both sides agreeing to withdraw their troops. Finally, in 1842, the boundary dispute was at length settled by the treaty signed by Queen Victoria's special envoy, Lord Ashburton, and Daniel Webster, our Secretary of State.

Both men had links with Maine. Webster as a young man had been preceptor of Fryeburg Academy, and Lord Ashburton had an American wife who had special property interests in Maine. She was a daughter of William Bingham, a wealthy merchant and banker of Philadelphia, after whom Bingham, Maine, and Binghamton, New York, were named. He owned two million acres of land in Maine. Two of his daughters married the brothers, Alexander and Henry Baring, of the great English banking house of that name. Alexander Baring became a peer of the realm, with the title of Lord Ashburton. The town of Baring, Maine, was named for him.

The bloodless Aroostook War stimulated the settlement of the eastern boundary lands, many farmers moving in from southern Maine. The farmers found that the forest loam where the timber had been cut was rich and perfectly adapted to growing potatoes, but this natural advantage was largely offset by the lack of transportation facilities. Starch factories were built to which most of the potato crop went, but this was not enough to warrant agricultural expansion on a large scale, and the area developed slowly.

In 1862 there was great rejoicing in the frontier villages up and down the line when the New Brunswick Railway, now part of the Canadian Pacific system, constructed a branch line from Saint Andrews to a point five miles from Houlton, which several years later was continued into the town. This gave the region an outlet through Canada to markets to the south. It was encouraging, but the situation was still far from satisfactory, and it wasn't until the building of the Bangor and Aroostook Railroad in the nineties that the land really flowered extensively with the white and purple blossoms of the potato.

In 1890, when the idea of a railroad for Aroostook County was conceived and began to be talked about, the region was still half wild and sparsely settled. Potato production was estimated at not more than a million bushels. But the railroad planners saw possibilities for development, and were willing to back their faith in Aroostook County with their private fortunes. Maine, it is interesting to note, was among the pioneer railroad-building states. The first railroad in the state and one of the first in the country was the Bangor, Old Town, and Milford Railroad, completed in 1836.

The Bangor and Aroostook Railroad was organized in 1891 by a group of Maine men led by Albert A. Burleigh of Houlton and Franklin W. Cram of Bangor. Construction began the following year and the first trains were operated in 1894. It was a period of acute financial depression, and it was only by pledging their personal credit, by the pledging of the credit of Aroostook County, and the support of the international banking house of Brown Brothers that they were able to put through the project and open up what was then largely virgin territory.

Economically, Aroostook County was dependent on the railroad and vice versa, and both progressed to a remarkable degree. By 1900 three hundred and fifty-four miles of the railroad had been built. The valuation of estates in northern Maine had doubled, potato production had increased fivefold, and the output of forest products was twice what it had been.

During the next decade the railroad built branch lines through various parts of the area which it served, and a line to the harbors of Searsport and Stockton Springs on Penobscot Bay, giving Aroostook County a tidewater outlet where deep-draught vessels could load. This practically completed the Bangor and Aroostook system.

Climate, soil, and the Bangor and Aroostook Railroad were the vital and indispensable factors in creating the potato paradise. Yet without the spirit and energy which the people of the region showed in taking advantage of their opportunities, it would still be more or less of a backwoods place.

The climate of these northern latitudes, with its bright warm days and cool nights and abundant rainfall, is ideal for potato growing. The summer season is short, but under the prevailing conditions the crop matures rapidly. The deep, well-drained soil produces such bumper crops that Aroostook County ranks first in the country in the number of bushels produced per acre.

The potato statistics for the county are not uninteresting. In 1946 Aroostook had an acreage of 196,500 out of the state's total of 219,000 acres. The entire state crop was 77,745,000 bushels, of which 71,133,000 were grown in Aroostook County, where the yield was 362 bushels per acre—a figure which has been surpassed both before and since.

But it is not enough just to grow a lot of potatoes. They must also be good. The Maine product is of such outstanding quality that it is in demand not only for consumption but for seed as well. Thirty-five potato-producing states and several foreign countries use certified Maine potato seed. Science has, of course, helped to better the stock and eliminate disease. In the starch factories, fewer potatoes are now required to produce starch than was formerly the case.

It was the old-time Yankee skipper in his small coastwise vessel who did much to spread the fame of the Maine potato. If he could get a few barrels of potatoes, a few barrels of apples, and few bundles of cedar shingles, he would sail south and with his genius for trading usually do pretty well. It was the dryness and flavor of the Maine potato that people liked.

In its issue of November 2, 1848, the Bangor *Whig and Courier* reported that a Maine vessel with a cargo of five hundred barrels of potatoes had arrived at New Orleans, where the potatoes were selling for fifty cents a dozen or nine dollars a barrel.

Exactly one hundred years later Maine was exporting potatoes to Europe. Overseas shipments from the Bangor and Aroostook Railroad potato terminal at Searsport amounted to nearly eight thousand carloads, more than half destined for Germany, the rest for France, Italy, and Greece. In addition hundreds of carloads were sent by sea from this point to southern Atlantic ports, including Norfolk, Savannah, and Jacksonville, which shows that Maine still uses the water route to get some of her products to market. In quantity and value, Maine's potato crop exceeds those of her sea and shore fisheries, large as they are. The potato crop amounts to between fifteen and twenty per cent of the whole United States output.

In developing Aroostook County an interesting experiment in colonization was made in 1870, when a company of Swedish immigrants was induced to come to this country to settle in the northern wilderness near Caribou. During the middle of the nineteenth century, the state had become alarmed at the number of people who were migrating from Maine to the West, and as the movement continued after the Civil War, William Widgery Thomas, Jr., who had been United States Consul at Gothenburg, Sweden, was appointed a commissioner to visit that country and obtain twenty-five families to settle in a town which had been set apart for them in Aroostook County. He was successful, and on July 23, 1870, the immigrants reached their new home which they called New Sweden.

The colony consisted of twenty-two men, eleven women, and eighteen children, a total of fifty-one. Others followed from Sweden and before the end of the year the number had increased to one hundred and fourteen. During the first decade, the colonists, whose numbers increased so that they spilled over into the territory adjacent to New Sweden, cleared 4,438 acres of wild land, built a church, a town house, five schoolhouses, three mills, one hundred and sixty-three dwellings, one hundred and fifty-one barns, and had also constructed forty-two and one-half miles of road. Today New Sweden and its neighbor Stockholm are prosperous potato-farming communities whose inhabitants are chiefly descendants of the original Scandinavian settlers.

At the time the Swedish pioneers arrived, the settled parts of Aroostook were chiefly along the eastern boundary, the section that has always been best suited to potato growing. From the fringes of the plantations the vast forest then ran back with scarcely a break to the shores of the St. Lawrence. In this great expanse of woods, moose and other game were plentiful, and large herds of caribou ranged the country. Moose, now protected, still roam through the remoter parts, but the caribou has disappeared. The local name for the rich Aroostook earth that produces bumper crops of potatoes is "caribou soil."

The town of Caribou, near New Sweden, is the potato metropolis of northeastern Aroostook. Here, as at other shipping centers, huge warehouses stand beside the railroad tracks, where the potatoes are sorted, graded, and stored. Despite the enormous capacity of the warehouses, it is sometimes inadequate to meet all requirements. In 1943 the crop was so great that millions of bushels had to be stored in sheds, barns, cellars, dwellings, and even in church basements. To avoid loss of this surplus, the farmers appealed to the government, and many trainloads of potatoes were removed to storage places outside the state.

At harvest time Aroostook County is invaded by an army of pickers, part of the floating population of American workers who move from one part of the country to another as various crops mature. These harvest hands are housed and fed and paid by the barrel for what they pick. It is only necessary to ride through the potato country and see fields stretching to the horizon to get an inkling of the amount of labor involved in harvesting the crop. As in all agricultural communities, the chief topic of conversation among the farmers during the growing and harvesting seasons concerns the market. How much will the crop bring? The potato industry has its ups and downs of fortune.

IN THE old days when you could get a whole township in Maine for less than a song, certain conditions were generally made a part of the grant. Settlement had to be made within a specified time, and each settler was required to build a house and clear a certain amount of land. This did not mean that a man to perfect his title had only to chop down a few trees and build himself a habitation scarcely larger than a rabbit hutch. The size of the

129

house and the number of acres to be cleared were usually specified.

Thus the town of Standish in Cumberland County was granted to Captain Humphrey Hobbs, and Captain Moses Pearson and their military companies for services at the siege of Louisburg. The whole number of grantees was to be one hundred and twenty, half of whom were to settle in separate families within three years, the remainder within seven years. They were to give bonds to the treasurer of the province that each man would build a log house sixteen by eighteen feet, and clear five acres of land.

Even in the early days there were men who made a business of building and selling rough wilderness homes. The pioneer settler in the town of Mercer, near the Belgrade Lakes, was a Revolutionary soldier named Nathaniel Emery. The first homes here were built along the Sandy River, amid noble growths of maple, elm, butternut, and other hardwoods. Visible today on an old granite millstone near the church in Mercer is a plate commemorating what is thought to have been America's largest elm. It had a girth of thirty-two feet, which is two feet bigger than the country's greatest living elm at Wethersfield, Connecticut. It was Nathaniel Emery's practice to fell a few acres of trees, build a log cabin, and sell the place with the improve-

ments to some newcomer. He would then begin
again.

A century or so later some remarkably fine log
houses were built by the Swedes who settled the
town of New Sweden in Aroostook County in 1870.
One of the better class of houses there, which
showed the Swedish style of building, was described in 1878 as follows:

"It is built of hewn logs, clap-boarded, with the
interstices between the logs calked with moss—a
warm and solid building. The plan of the house
struck us as being very convenient. The entrance
hall does not run through the building, but nearly
across the front, having little depth, but considerable length. In the rear of the hall, opposite the
outer door, entrance is given to a large, square re-
ception-room, which occupies the middle of the
house. On each side of this are two smaller rooms,
entrance to which is gained from the hall, and also
from the central room. These smaller rooms are
used as kitchen, sitting-room and bed-rooms."

When frame dwellings began to be erected, the
building of a house was a social event. All the
neighbors turned out for the raising. The frame was
pegged together and many hands helped to raise
it into place. The work was done gratuitously, but
the owner was expected to supply plenty of liquid
refreshment. Rum was then the popular drink. A
gallon sufficed to raise a one-story house. Twice that

amount was required if it was a two-story structure. Half a dozen bucketfuls would raise a house, ell, and barn, but if the owner was well-to-do it took more. No less than a barrelful was required to raise a meetinghouse. "Rarin' the meetin' house," it was called.

The rum was generally taken straight, but if the building was a public one, which always drew a crowd, rum punch was served. The old Maine formula for this mixture was one sour, two sweet, four strong, eight weak.

When the frame had been raised the ancient custom of naming it was observed. This took the form of a dialogue between a couple of lads perched at opposite ends of the ridgepole, one of whom would say to the other, "Here is a fine frame without a name. What shall we call it?" Questions and answers followed until the frame was named. Frequently the branch of an evergreen or other tree was affixed to the ridgepole as a triumphal note. Three cheers were then given, and after a parting cup the people went home rejoicing.

Few houses built during the first century of the colonial period have survived in Maine, but this is not strange considering all the destruction that occurred during the French and Indian wars, when many settlements were wiped out and Maine was largely abandoned to the enemy. The oldest settled parts of the state lie along the seaboard and the principal rivers, and it is here that one sees the most imposing examples of late eighteenth- and early nineteenth-century architecture. It was a period of intense marine activity, when almost everybody was concerned either directly or indirectly with the business of going to sea in ships. Sea captains, ship owners, merchants, and lumbermen made fortunes, which enabled them to build the substantial homes that grace the coastal towns from Kittery to Belfast and beyond.

Building such houses was by no means confined to the towns. Maine's waterfront measures some twenty-four hundred miles in length, and you are likely to find gracious and charming old houses almost anywhere along the line. Today many of these places seem remote and isolated, but they were built in the days when the sea figured importantly in the lives of the people, and there was good reason for building them where they did.

I remember driving along a lonely road and stopping to look at an old house standing empty and solitary in a field. There were good lines to her— in Maine they often speak of houses as they do of ships in the feminine gender—and she was well preserved. There was a sturdy, squat chimney, and a fine front door, with fluted pilasters at the sides and a graceful fanlight overhead. As I approached the house, it was soon apparent why it had been built in that particular spot. From the road you

could not see that the property sloped down to the
arm of a bay which here made far up into the land.
I had not even suspected the presence of any water
so near at hand. On the shore below the house was
the ruin of an old stone wharf. The history of the
place in its broader outlines immediately became
clear. Nor was it difficult to imagine what life here
had been like.

Old landmarks of this kind are to be met with in
many out-of-the-way places all along the coast. Of
substantial but not extravagant size, sensibly
planned and strongly built, they were designed
with one end in view—the provision of comfort
and convenience for those they sheltered, as these
things were understood in the days when life was
less cluttered and distracting than it is today. I
have heard it said that a fine view and a sunny
aspect meant less to our forefathers than they do
to us, but seeing where and how the older generations built, inclines me to believe that these things
were as fully appreciated by them as by ourselves.
They were not insensible to the feeling that a good
house deserves an agreeable situation, or perhaps
it should be put the other way around.

Building fine houses came naturally to the people of Maine. They were shipbuilders acutely sen-
sitive to beauty of line and form, with a perceptive
eye for detail. They designed and built houses as
they did ships, with particular grace and excel-

lence. The traditional skill of Maine carpenters—
the inboard joiners and the outboard joiners, the
figurehead carvers and the ship smiths—may be
seen in a place like Wiscasset, which possesses perhaps as fine a collection of magnificent old houses
as any single town in Maine.

The houses were built in the golden years between 1790 and 1812, when the harbor was crowded with shipping, the trade of the port extended to
all parts of the world, and wealth poured into the
town. Many of the Georgian houses on High Street
and in other parts of the town which give Wiscasset
its atmosphere of antiquity were built during this
period. Individually the houses are of the greatest
interest. The spacious, high-ceilinged rooms, with
their fireplaces and panel work, have the old, mild
luster of the candlelight era. There is not one that
has not its special associations. There was a party
in progress at Major Moses Carlton's home the winter night in 1815 when the news reached Wiscasset
that the war was over. The Carlton house was the
only lighted one in town, and the messenger rode
his horse right into the hall to announce the news.

The Sortwell house is the most prominent feature of the village street that runs down the hill
from the common to the harbor. It attracts the attention of the traveler at once with its lofty front
and rich ornamental carving. It is said to have
taken two years to complete the front hall. This

grand house was built in 1807 and 1808 by Captain William Nickels, a retired shipmaster, who wanted a house in which he could entertain and spend his winter years in comfort. The scale on which it was planned is shown by its quota of fireplaces which kept one man busy supplying them with wood. After Captain Nickels' time the house was for many years an inn, but half a century ago it came into the possession of the Sortwell family, and has ever since been treated with the affectionate care it deserves.

One of the most curious old houses in Maine is that of Edbury Hatch in Newcastle. Born in that town in 1849, he was the last of the old ship figure-head carvers and his work is represented in a number of marine museums. As a boy he showed a good deal of aptitude for whittling and was apprenticed for four years to William Southworth, who carved hundreds of figureheads for Maine-built ships. Edbury decorated the exterior of the family homestead with elaborately carved designs. The three entrances to the house are heavily ornamented with his wood carvings, as is also the cupola. The pointed roof of the front porch is surmounted by a spread eagle mounted on a wooden ball supported by fancy scrollwork like the carved stern piece of a ship. Fretwork on either side of the porch rises to a pointed arch just below the eagle. The carving is, of course, ornate and extravagant, the kind of gingerbread work that was thought so much of during the last decades of the last century, but which people today look upon with amusement or dismay. But the handiwork of this master carver is unique.

Edbury Hatch carved many eagles for building ornaments, and he carved signs, too, one of which is over the entrance to the Newcastle firehouse. Local tradition says he made this sign, which shows a fireman's helmet, a speaking trumpet, an ax, a ladder, and other fire-fighting equipment, out of gratitude to the company of local volunteers for saving his house when one close to it burned. Besides figureheads and architectural ornaments, Edbury Hatch did a good deal with furniture, mirrors, hanging shelves, ship models, and bas-relief carvings of ships which, like his figureheads, he painted himself. One of these hangs in the library at Damariscotta, which also has his books, including one on carving from which he got some of his designs. Edbury Hatch became blind at the age of eighty-five, and it is only since his death a few years ago that his work has come to be appreciated.

In view of all the stone there is in Maine, it is surprising so little should have been used for construction purposes. Apart from a few ancient jails, lighthouses, and forts, old stone structures are rare in Maine. Only occasionally does one find a dwelling built of native stone. Quarrying in earlier times seems to have been confined mostly to the production of gravestones, millstones, grindstones, and whetstones.

The old York Gaol, built in 1653, is one of the oldest stone buildings in the state. The old walls and dungeon are concealed in a later structure—a large, gambrel-roofed house. It was for many years the only reasonably safe prison in Maine. When the notorious Henry Tufts almost succeeded in burning his way out of the Portland jail, he was taken to York for safekeeping. Prisoners in the old Maine jails, if they did not like the victuals, would threaten to leave if better fare were not provided, and sometimes they did depart without much difficulty.

The old Oxford County jail at Paris Hill, small, square, and somber, was built in 1828, but it is many years since any scoundrels or unfortunates have been detained within its massive walls. It has been a library for more than half a century, a memorial to Hannibal Hamlin, who was a Parisian by birth and enjoyed the distinction of being vice-president for one term under Abraham Lincoln.

Older, larger and less sullen, perhaps, is the aged jail on the hill overlooking the Sheepscot River at Wiscasset. It was built just before the War of 1812, and the prisoners taken by Commodore Tucker in the naval action off Pemaquid were lodged there. If stone walls do not a prison make, those of the Wiscasset jail give a very good imitation of one. All the stone jails of Maine emphatically look the part.

The courthouse in Wiscasset, which stands at the head of Maine Street, is a notable building. Built of brick, the marble keystone in the arch over the front entrance dates it, for it is inscribed "1824." This arch and those over the front windows are perfect. The brick dome above the front doors in the recessed entrance is a remarkable piece of brick-work. The courtroom, where cases are still heard, has not the bleak atmosphere of many old court-rooms, but is pleasant and dignified in what might be called a courtly way. It is a room rich in his-torical associations, for many famous lawyers have pleaded causes in Wiscasset, among them Daniel Webster and Jeremiah Mason.

Not far from Wiscasset is an old unworked gran-ite quarry. It is on the high northern entrance point to Round Pond on Muscongus Bay. To judge by the size of the excavation, a good deal of stone was taken from it in bygone days. This quarry probably accounts for the presence near the village of a stone schoolhouse, which has not been used as a school for many years. Probably the solidity of its con-struction has saved it from destruction. It was a schoolboy in another town in the same county as Round Pond and Wiscasset, who when asked to state some of the characteristics of the local rocks, said, "They are heavy as hell, they are hard as hell, and they hurt like hell when you drop one on your foot."

There is a fine old stone house on one of the islands lying out in Muscongus Bay near Round Pond. The island is one that would please a collector of islands, and the house a collector of houses. One end of the island, which is partly wooded, has a high, rocky shore, while the other end is sloping pasture land. The house stands on rising ground above the small harbor. New England farmhouse in style, its ells are stepped back to admit the light. A long period of emptiness has produced dereliction and decay. Sheep billeted on the island were wandering through the best rooms when I was there. Nobody seems to know how old it is, nor if the stone for it came from the Round Pond quarry. Mrs. Lyman Macfarland of New Harbor, who lived in the house as a girl, told me her family had occupied it a long time before her day, but she did not know how long. It is probably safe to say that the house is at least a centenarian. I never think of it without recalling James Thurber's motto, "Run, don't walk, to the nearest desert island."

Some old houses were built on granite foundations, the blocks of stone coming from some nearby quarry, but for the most part rough stone was used for cellar walls, only the steps being hewn. In houses of the central chimney type the masonry foundation for the chimney took up a lot of cellar room, the huge base rising to the ground floor sometimes measuring as much as ten feet square. Be-

cause of the poor quality of brick used, many of the
large chimneys had to be torn out, leaving only the
base in the cellar, and people, forgetting that there
ever was a central chimney, have been puzzled by
the mass of masonry under the middle of the house.
An old lady who lived on a hill where soldiers had
been stationed during the War of 1812 told me her
house was built over the old town powder magazine. I went to see it, but it was only the large
foundation for the chimney.

People on the coast do a good deal of moving—
not just the contents of houses, but the houses themselves. They move them from the islands to the
mainland and vice versa and from place to place
along the coast. A man will see a lonely old house
somewhere and feeling sorry for it will buy it and
move it where the old thing can enjoy the company
of other houses. Sometimes whole communities are
moved. When the granite quarry at Head Harbor
Island on Moosabec Reach was shut down, there
was a general exodus from the island, the people
taking their houses with them. They liked their
homes and did not wish to abandom them.

Maine has among its antiquities a number of interesting meetinghouses. Built in discreet traditional New England style, they command the respect and attention of everybody who is interested
in old buildings. The first meetinghouses were
nothing more than square log structures with steep

thatched roofs and only the bare earth for a floor. This type was followed as soon as the colonists could afford it by the second order of New England meetinghouse, which was a square frame building with a pyramidal roof topped by a cupola or turret, in which hung the bell if the town had one. Many meetinghouses were built in this architectural style in the seventeenth century. Then came the third form, the white meetinghouse with or without a steeple, which we now generally think of as the typical New England house of worship.

There is an interesting description of a church of this last order that stood for many years in New Gloucester in Cumberland County. The township was granted in 1735 to sixty inhabitants of Gloucester, Massachusetts, whence, of course, came the name. There were sixty-three shares, the odd three being as usual for the first minister, the support of the ministry, and the schools. Settlement began in 1742, when the household goods of the settlers were landed at the mouth of Royals River and poled up the stream on rafts. For several years during the French and Indian wars the settlement was abandoned. "The first meetinghouse was built in 1770, and stood until 1838. It was a quaint but ambitious edifice. It had a square tower on the southwest end, and a porch on the other. Twenty-six windows in two rows let in the light through their eight by ten panes. Galleries on three sides rose to the height of the preacher's eyes, as he stood in the lofty pulpit under the threatening sounding-board. Wardens with long staffs watched for sleepers, and sometimes the reminder of the knobbed end was far from gentle. Holes in the floors served for spittoons, and gave ample ventilation. Seats turned up on their hinges during prayer to afford space for the wide skirts of the ladies, and dropped down with a rattling chorus and many a bang at the welcome 'Amen.' The town's stock of powder was kept in small closets within the sacred desk, ready to be served out to the members of the congregation on Sundays and at their homes on secular days, in case of Indian attack."

Since meetinghouses were unheated in those days, they were, in spite of the hell-fire-and-brimstone sermons preached in them, about as safe as any place for storing powder. But powder or no powder, during a thunderstorm the service was suspended and the congregation went outside to take refuge under the trees.

Of surviving examples of eighteenth-century meetinghouses, probably the best known is the Unitarian Church in Kennebunk, which was built in 1774 and sympathetically remodeled a quarter of a century or so later. It has a splendid steeple with an open belfry above which is a public clock, and over that an octagonal cupola wherein a lantern could be hung. The steeple rises from a tall square tower in which is the front entrance. It is in old steeples like this that one can see examples of the ingenious work of the old-time carpenters. Oak and chestnut were commonly used for steeple beams.

The old white church at York is another fine example of an eighteenth-century religious edifice. It has a tall, slender spire tipped by a weathercock. Built in 1747, this meetinghouse did not originally face the street, but stood broadside to it. It was turned and certain renovations and alterations made. Shortly after it was struck by lightning, which was looked upon by those who had opposed the changes as a mark of divine displeasure visited on those who were responsible for them.

Of a different type is the meetinghouse at Alna on the Sheepscot River. The exterior of this weathered building, which was erected the year George Washington became the first president, is almost as plain and severe as a barn, but inside the design and workmanship are more elaborate. There are galleries on three sides with tiered box pews, but as in the case of most old meetinghouses of this type, the decoration is chiefly centered in the high paneled pulpit, with its winding stairway leading to the platform and desk, and the octagonal canopy or sounding board suspended over it.

These sounding boards in the old churches were more ornamental than useful, though they were thought to be necessary and helpful to the parson when he preached. But their effect was to stifle the sound of his voice. They prevented him from making the rafters ring. So far as I know there is no record of one's falling on a preacher and silencing him completely, though doubtless on many a Sunday morning children bored by the long sermon hoped it would come crashing down.

Most Maine architecture is anonymous. In some instances wealthy people employed architects from Boston and other places to design their mansions. Nicholas Codd and Alexander Pariss of Boston are both believed to have done work for Maine clients. The famous Ruggles house at Columbia Falls was designed and built in 1819 by Aaron Sherman, the carpenter-architect of Duxbury, Massachusetts. But for the most part Maine homes, from the largest to the humblest, were entirely the work of local craftsmen. The old houses stand as a monument to their traditional skill in design and workmanship.

SPRING in its northward progress enters Maine
by way of the highway bridge across the Piscataqua
River between Portsmouth, New Hampshire, and
Kittery, Maine. This is the processional route. Once
across the river the season advances steadily along
the coast, deploying its forces left and right, reaching up into the interior and down to the fingertips
of the long peninsulas, whence it jumps from island
to island. The coast blossoms a week or so in ad-

146

vance of the interior and ten days to two weeks
ahead of the islands, but the latter make up for
this later in the year, as they are not touched by
frost so early as the coast. Visitors to the offshore
islands have been surprised to find autumn gardens
flourishing a fortnight after all the mainland flowers have perished. So swiftly does the season move
that, barring unexpected setbacks, the whole revolutionary process is over in a couple of weeks.
When spring comes, Maine knows the summer
people are not far behind.

Visitors from the southern half of New England
and from New York, New Jersey, and Pennsylvania who go to Maine early in the summer are
twice blessed, for the season is less advanced in
Maine and they can experience the pleasures
of spring at home and enjoy an extension of it
in Maine. When elsewhere lilacs have ceased to
bloom, peonies dropped, and ramblers faded, they
are at their best in Maine. People have for centuries
been thrilled by the sight and scent of Maine in
spring and summer.

"So pleasant a scene here they had as did much
refresh them," wrote John Winthrop, "and there
came a smell off the land like the smell of a garden."

This was on June 8, 1630, when a fleet of fourteen
vessels bound for Massachusetts Bay came on the
coast at Mount Desert. Crossing the Atlantic was

then not a matter of days but of weeks which sometimes became months, and to have made the landfall of Mount Desert, the highest and handsomest island on the coast, must have been very heartening to these New England voyagers in their cramped and crowded ships. The smell of the land after long days at sea always acts as a pleasant restorative.

Throughout most of its length the Maine coast is a flower garden. All summer long wherever you go you are in the presence of flowers. Meadows, woods, roadsides, and even ditches are favored with them. In June and July fields and pastures are yellow with paintbrush, while along the roadsides daisies and purple vetch are outstanding. Near the water clusters of wild roses glow with brilliant hues. Then there are the gardens. Even the most dreadful little shack has its flowers.

Like other New Englanders, the people of Maine are extremely fond of lilacs, which in spring bloom in dooryards everywhere. The lilac is so typically American in its associations that it is difficult to realize that it was brought by an old Himalayan traveler from High Asia, and did not reach New England until the middle of the eighteenth century. Maine missed by a narrow margin being the original home of the flower in this country. For the first lilacs in America are believed to have been those planted just across the Piscataqua River in Portsmouth, New Hampshire, by Governor Benning Wentworth, when he was made chief magistrate in 1750. That year he added a council chamber and other rooms and a terrace to the house which his father had built half a century earlier, making a snug dwelling of forty rooms, with ample stabling for a score or more of horses in the cellar. The lilacs which came from England were used in landscaping the gubernatorial mansion. Tradition says that those which George Washington planted at Mount Vernon were from slips taken from the Wentworth lilacs. In any case, the purple lilac is the official flower of Maine's next-door neighbor.

Occasionally one sees a one-color garden in Maine. I know of an all-blue spring garden and an all-white summer garden. White is the color that carries farthest, particularly when seen against a deeper background. Who it was that first saw the value of gray and silvery foliage for borders I know not, but I dare say it was some woman with an artist's eye for color and a flair for pictorial gardening. Gray and frosted silver tones give value, by close association, to the more delicate shades of blue, pink, lilac, and, above all, white. There was an abundance of it in the two single-color gardens mentioned.   .

There are said to be fifty shades of green, and the best is the green of Maine apple trees, which one often sees in the vicinity of gardens in Southwestern Maine.

One likes the forthright honesty of Maine gardeners. A plant may be common, but if it does well and the color is right, they are not afraid to use it. This is not to say that there are no gardeners of odd and subtle tastes in Maine, but that gardens of the less sophisticated and simpler order seem to go very well with the old houses.

Looking back on my gardening days in Maine it seems as if I was always transplanting, moving plants from places where they had done only fairly well to places where I thought they might do better; shifting others which seemed to occupy more space than they deserved to make room for things worthier of a better hole, and giving space to new plants I had not had before. Too much of this, too little of that, and gaps in the succession of blooms. In every garden you have to consider the past, the present, and the future.

In Maine gardens you are apt to see flowers which are so old-fashioned that they no longer find a place in seed catalogues—bee balm and scilla, for example. Outside the Wiscasset Library they used to have Solomon's-seal, and in the Berry's garden near by the tall red flower, Maltese cross. The most unusual garden in Wiscasset lies next to the main street, but you cannot see it, as it is in the cellar hole of the old inn that stood next to the Sortwell house. You descend into this sunken garden by the original stone stairs. The deep foundation walls are composed of blocks of gray granite which make an admirable background for the borders. The flower I remember best in this garden was the globe thistle. The tall plants with their spiny grayish leaves and the round heads of the steely blue flowers made an interesting note among the other midsummer plants.

Quite a different kind of garden was that of the late Mrs. Charles Orne of West Boothbay Harbor, where the Orne family has a general store and at one time had the post office. The store stands by the harborside close to a high retaining wall, and on the terrace between the store and the edge of the wall Mrs. Orne had a garden practically overhanging the water. It was a real seaside garden. It was small, but many of the flowers were to be seen against the water, and it was delightful. Once while waiting for some children who were in the store buying checkerberry candy and popcorn cakes, I walked around to look at the garden, and Mrs. Orne came out and picked me a bouquet of poppies and babies'-breath to take home. The poppies were the intense color that only the sea air can give them.

Maine has many garden traditions, but fortunately the custom of having gnomes in gardens has not taken hold. They are perhaps tolerable in gardens that are the haunt of children, who often delight in them, though there are other garden orna-

ments that seem more desirable than these face-
tious little men. Perhaps Maine gardeners have discovered that the phrase "gnomes in gardens" works
out as an anagram into "Gad, grim nonsense!"

Apart from the more sinister orchids, there are
few flowers which can startle one with their fan-
tastic unreality quite as much as the tuberous-
rooted begonias. They do not seem real at all, but
rather the invention of some artist, though they are,
of course, as actual and authentic as daisies and
buttercups. They thrive in the shade and like moist,
sandy soil. They do well on the north side of buildings and hedges or in places where most of the sunlight is cut off by trees or other growth. The climate
and soil of Maine are especially well suited to growing them, particularly along the coast, and above all
on the islands.

For many years Howard R. Rich made a business
of growing begonias on Swan's Island off Blue Hill
Bay, shipping tubers to all parts of the country.
Commercial growers raise them in lath houses
which give the plants the proper amount of light
and shade and the necessary air circulation. One
reads of the rich and cruel colors of the jungle, but
in August and September when the begonias on
Swan's Island are in bloom they make the tropic
hues look dull. These exotic flowers came to this
country from Bolivia by way of England, but they
have been vastly improved since they left their na-

tive home, until now they appear in a great variety of forms, colors, and shades.

Swan's Island, incidentally, abounds in purple-fringed orchis, and wild calla lilies are found on near-by Great Cranberry Island.

The fondness which Maine people have for begonias is evident from the number which you see. Very noticeable are the window boxes filled with them in Damariscotta. They seem to be mostly the camelia type, with large, six-inch blossoms in the most gorgeous colors—salmon, pink, rose, apricot, orange, scarlet, yellow, and white. The woman who runs the greenhouse near the cemetery in Damariscotta produces and sells them reasonably. Her name is Boynton, but she calls her place Few-acres, and is always amused when people address her as Mrs. Fewacres. The first begonias I had in Maine came from her, and they did well, except that I made the mistake of giving them too much water, and they dropped their blossoms. The last time I was at this greenhouse was on June 6, 1944. There had been an unusual and severe frost the night before. Like greenhouse owners everywhere during the war, Mrs. Boynton had gone in heavily for vegetable plants for the local Victory gardens and had no begonias, or, at any rate, none left for me. Behind her greenhouse she had many tomato plants and these were desolated. The frost got eight thousand of them. It was reminiscent of the year eighteen-hundred-and-froze-to-death (1817), when unseasonal frosts throughout New England caused a great exodus of people to Ohio, including fifteen thousand from Maine.

Window boxes filled with flowers help any place. Even if you have no garden you can get a good effect with them, and they look well from inside the house as well as outside. By using greenhouse plants you can get immediate results. I recollect filling one box which was over six feet long with pink geraniums, the trailing kind of lobelia, which is, of course, intensely blue and does well in Maine, white petunias, and inch plant or wandering Jew. It was an effective combination.

A garden is worth having if for no other reason than to attract birds. Almost any kind of a garden will do for this purpose, though certain flowers attract certain birds. Hummingbirds, of course, like tubular flowers, as they normally live on nectar and small insects, both of which are gathered from the inner recesses of the blossoms. To reach this food supply the bird has not only a long bill but also an extremely extensile tongue. The tongue, which has a piston-like action, is a remarkable piece of mechanism. The spring-like roots pass behind the bird's ear openings, over the top of its head, and find anchorage between the eyes.

By including petunias in the planting of the window box just mentioned, I was able for several sea-

sons to get a good view of these living gems feeding
on the wing, as they invariably do, only a few feet
from me. The sunlight reaching the box early in
the morning did full justice to their superb metallic
colors. The male and female were easily distin-
guishable by the absence of any ruby from the
throat of the female. The feverish activity of the
birds continued intermittently from early morning,
until late in the evening. Only occasionally did one
take time out and pause to survey the garden from
a bare branch at the top of the crab apple tree or
from the light-wire. With its long bill and short
tail, it looked at such times rather like a tiny king-
fisher. But it never rested long. Suddenly it would
dart off on a direct line of flight, presumably to its
nest, and would stay away for awhile. Hummingbirds in my experience are late stayers in Maine.
I have known them to remain until the first week
in October, when though the days were still mild,
the nights were chilly. It may be that they stay as
long as there are any flowers left for them to pil-
lage.

During the War of 1812, while Castine was occupied by the enemy, a coastal character named
Hatevil Colson asked a British captain if he had
ever seen any Yankee hummingbirds. The officer
said he never had, and Colson promised to bring
him some. "They're fine singers," he added. Colson had been a wanderer along the coast for years,

particularly around the Penobscot Bay area. He was an amiable tramp who was welcome everywhere he went because of his unfailing wit and his willingness to do anything for anybody. People gave the usual romantic explanation of his nomadism: that is, early disappointment in love. Actually, he was something of a hero, a horseless Paul Revere, who made his way through the woods to warn Belfast and the Penobscot River towns that the British were coming.

Not long after Hate had spoken to the British officer he appeared with a wasps' nest plugged at the end, which he said was a nest of hummingbirds. Now such a nest was as unfamiliar to the British as were the birds alleged to be inside, and they suspected nothing. John Josselyn, it will be recalled, who visited Maine in 1638, had an adventure with a wasps' nest. In his *New England's Rareities Discovered* he tells how, while out for a walk at Scarborough in quest of curiosities, he found a nest which in his ignorance he took hold of and was stung beyond recognition. "The wasps breed in hives made like a great pineapple," he wrote afterward; "their entrance is at the lower end, the whole hive is of an ash color, but of what matter it's made no man knows. Wax it is not, neither will it melt or fry, but will take fire suddenly like tinder." Longfellow, remembering Josselyn's experience with the wasps, wrote:

I feel like Master Josselyn when he found
The hornets' nest, and thought it some strange
    fruit,
Until the seeds came out, and then he dropped
    it.

Colson told the British that if they wished to
hear the birds sing they must shut themselves up in
a room with all cracks and crevices sealed and the
keyhole stuffed. In accordance with these instructions, the officer and his friends took the strange
nest out to one of the warships anchored in Castine
Harbor and secluded themselves in one of the cab-
ins. The nest was then opened and given a stir and
the birds began to sing, very angrily and unpleas-
antly. They swarmed out of the nest and went for
the British officers. Not a man at the concert escaped
being badly stung. Afterwards they looked for Colson, but he had disappeared, and though searching
parties scoured the countryside for him, he could
not be found. The Yankee practical joker had vanished in the woods.

Since hummingbirds feed on the wing it is a
matter of indifference to them whether you have a
lawn or not, but other garden birds are attracted
by one. It gives them a treadable surface across
which they can run, a thing they could not do were
the grass long, and it also provides them with a
well-stocked feeding ground, though most of the

provender lies beneath the surface. Among the birds which used to visit my brief patch of lawn were three or four pairs of robins who brought their young with them, but never more than one or two at a time. It made me wonder if they had left the others at home in the nest, or if the rest of the brood had fallen prey to other birds or animals. Whatever the answer, it was amusing to watch the fledglings that did come. At first they had no luck at all getting food, except occasionally something lying on the surface, but they soon learned. One of the attractions of birds is that everybody sees something individual in them, and anyone at any time may see something no one else has ever seen before.

Besides the lawn there was other grass to be cut, but a scythe is an implement I never learned the art of using properly. I soon discovered that it requires more skill to cut some grasses than others, but the expert mows them all with the same cleanness. It is easier to cut coarse grass, for example, than the delicate kind that lies down. One elderly man who did some mowing for me said he always ground his scythe more on the top than on the bottom, as it enabled him to cut the grass closer. There is a good deal of rhythm connected with the business of scything—rhythm in drawing the whetstone and laying it to the blade and rhythm in swinging the scythe. The sound of the whetstone and the swish of the blade through the grass are extremely pleasant. The swaying of the arms and body are as rhythmic as the movements of a rower. It is a fascinating thing to watch.

Maine's champion scyther was Richard Hunniwell of Scarborough who once fought an Indian in single combat with a scythe and beheaded the savage. Hunniwell was a famous Indian killer whom the redskins hated and feared. They had murdered his wife and child and Hunniwell had sworn vengeance. In war or peace he would kill any Indian whenever he had the opportunity. One day while he was mowing, an Indian tried to sneak up on him. He spotted the skulker, but pretended he had not seen him, and kept on cutting his swath toward the place where the Indian lay concealed. When within striking distance he suddenly bounded forward, which so surprised and disconcerted the Indian that he missed his aim, and with one terrific swipe Hunniwell lopped off his head. He then stuck the head on the end of a pole and set it up, so that the Indians on the other side of the swamp could see it, and bade them come on; but fearful that he would mow them all down, they withdrew. They finally got him, however, with twelve others, in a bloody battle near what came to be known as Massacre Pond. Hunniwell was a bonny fighter.

The Indians had an extensive and peculiar knowledge of herbs, particularly those of a medicinal kind, and a good deal of their knowledge was transmitted to and used by the settlers. A famous Penobscot Indian doctor was Big Thunder in whom even the whites appear to have placed some confidence. On Indiantown Island in the Sheepscot River is the traditional site of an Indian herb garden. As mentioned elsewhere, this island was a popular place of resort for the Indians in summer, and if they did not grow herbs there, they probably cultivated it for other purposes, because it is a natural place for a garden. It can be seen from the water, a tract several acres in extent, fully protected from the north and with a splendid southern exposure.

It is perhaps not altogether irrelevant to mention that before Maine became a state in 1820, Massachusetts granted a township near Houlton, in what is now Aroostook County, to endow a professorship of botany, and the town was named for the famous Swedish botanist, Karl von Linné (1707–1778), who is better known under the Latinized form of his name, Linnaeus. He was the great classifier. His object was to systematize the known species of plants and animals, and to describe them in scientific terms. He had extraordinary success and influence. Although modern taxonomists, or classifiers, pursuing a task that seems to be endless, may seek today to modify his system, their respect for his remarkable basic work remains undimmed. Maine cherishes the name and tradition of the great naturalist in the town of Linneus.

The world's first garden is also remembered in the name of another Maine town—Eden on Mount Desert Island. Although it is sometimes stated that the place was named for Richard Eden, an obscure sixteenth-century translator and author, there is a strong local tradition that the name was suggested by the natural beauties of the locality. Some people, seeing a descriptive name of this kind on the map, immediately jump to the conclusion that it was bestowed by some satirist, but in this particular case the name is not inappropriate.

TO TAKE PLEASURE IN
HARBORS AND COVES

THE COAST of Maine is honeycombed with countless coves and harbors. Many of them belong to the mainland, others to the islands. The poet Whittier did not exaggerate when he spoke of "hundred-harbored Maine." On the contrary, the truth warranted his placing the total at many times that figure. Probably nobody knows exactly how many there are, but an idea of the eccentric character of the coast is gained by recalling that, while the towns of Eastport and Lubec stand within sight of each other across a three-mile stretch of water, the distance between them by the shore line is one hundred miles.

Many of these little Maine harbors are fishing ports with small villages, dominated by a church, curving around them, but many more are deserted save by the sea birds that patrol them lazily, and nowadays are seldom visited except, perhaps, by fishermen who may camp there briefly during the summer. Sometimes you see an old house standing at the head of a cove, the original owner of which farmed and fished or went on trading voyages, but no vessel is moored in the haven now; and in many places the house, too, is gone.

It is a continuously interesting experience to live beside one of these coves. No two are alike, but they all share a certain common element. At least that is what I found, and I have spent some time beside several of them. One was Hodgdon's Cove at West Boothbay Harbor. There is high land all around it and woods and fields.

Like the play within the play of *Hamlet*, there is a cove within the cove, or since it is only a small indentation between two high wooded points, it is perhaps more reasonable to speak of it as a nook or alcove. Anyway, years ago a superannuated two-master was brought in here to die. She was old and leaky and soon sank. She had the spars in her when she first came in, but these went by the board. At high tide the wreck of the ancient schooner is mercifully covered, but when the tide ebbs she slowly emerges like a ghost wrapped in a shroud of brown seaweed.

From Alden Swett, who has been a cove resident for many years, I learned that she was the *Mary Ann,* and in her old age she was moored off the cove for shore dinners, but for one season only. It cost too much to keep her afloat. The gas engines had to be run constantly to prevent her sinking, so she was abandoned. In many other coves up and down the coast similar relics of the days of sail are moldering away.

Leslie Mello, who also lives at the cove, told me of another showboat that formerly operated along the coast forty years or more ago. Like the *Mary Ann,* she was a two-masted schooner. She used to come into Blue Hill where he lived in his younger days. The vessel had a crew of three or four men and carried a merry-go-round, which they unloaded and hauled to the fair grounds. There was a steam engine to run it. Music was furnished by a contraption of horns that played automatically. It took half a day to set up the merry-go-round. The fair lasted two days.

"There were thirty pairs of horses and two or three sleighs for elderly people," Leslie said. "All the horses were different—roans, dapple grays, and coal blacks. They moved up and down like rocking horses as the merry-go-round went around. The vessel used to visit Frankfort, Hall's Quarry, Stonington, and such places. The quarries were running then."

Later, when I asked Captain Ralph Frye of Northeast Harbor if he recalled the old merry-go-round vessel, he said, "Yes, I remember her. Can't recall her name, but my cousin Frank Saunders of Lubec was on her. One winter they went to Cuba, but they had a lot of trouble with them natives down there."

"Is Frank Saunders living?" I asked.

"No," he replied, "Frank died a few years ago. Don't know who the others were."

People were as keen to be entertained in bygone days as they are today, though they had far fewer opportunities to satisfy the yearning. When a good entertainment did come their way they were enthusiastic. Here is the notice of a performance from the *Boothbay Register* for July 20, 1878, which makes interesting reading today.

"On Tuesday and Wednesday evenings the citizens of Boothbay enjoyed a musical treat of rare excellence. The Bohemian Bell Ringers produced some of the finest music ever heard in Boothbay. Aside from the programme of the whole company on the bells which was to us truly astonishing, Miss Louise Scaffer's performance on the Cornet we have heard pronounced by several cornet players to be the best they ever heard, and some of her parts the most difficult they ever saw attempted. Her performance on the glass goblets was indeed marvelous. The clear ringing sound pervaded every part of the hall and held the audience in breathless suspense. Mr. Oscar Slater is not surpassed as a delineator of humorous character, especially as a hypochondriac. Mr. J. E. Masters' representations of the Heathen Chinee brought down the house. He seemed able to bring music from every instrument he touched, no matter how unmusical its appearance. Misses Sampson and Livingstone are artists who performed their parts to the satisfaction of the audience, and the whole company by their pleasant and social manners, as well as musical ability, left behind them pleasant remembrances to all who heard their performance."

Occasionally small yachts come into the cove, anchoring just inside the entrance when conditions are unfavorable for cruising, or during fine weather they come in to lie overnight. Over on Southport Island, directly opposite the cove, is a wharf with a store on it, where supplies can be obtained. This store is well known to boat owners and week-end mariners who are familiar with Townsend Gut. It was run for more than fifty years by Howard McKown.

Pleasure cruising on the coast of Maine is no new

thing. It has been going on for more than a century, and the old accounts make agreeable reading. One reason is that while sailing craft have changed, the character of the people who like to be afloat has altered very little, and the sea not at all.

In the summer of 1858, one of these pleasure craft with a number of young men aboard came down through Townsend Gut past the cove and swung around into Boothbay Harbor, where they lay over the week end. Among the company was Robert Carter, Washington correspondent of the *New York Tribune,* who wrote an interesting account of the voyage in a book called *A Summer Cruise on the New England Coast,* published in 1865.

He relates that on Sunday morning while they were lounging on deck reading the papers, a boat from the town came alongside with one man in it, a respectable looking person, who produced an empty bottle and asked them if he could have a little brandy, for which he would pay. He said his wife was sick, and the doctor had prescribed brandy, but none was to be had in the town.

They gave him a couple of bottles of ale, assuring him that he would have been welcome to the brandy if they had had any, but unfortunately they were out of everything of the kind. Presently they were hailed by a boat approaching from another quarter of the town. This, too, contained a single individual, and he too produced a bottle, and, strange to say, he likewise had a sick wife, for whom the doctor had prescribed brandy.

"I say, my dear fellow, are all the women in Boothbay sick and has the doctor prescribed brandy for all of them? You're the second chap who has been here within ten minutes with the same story. Hadn't you better call a town meeting, and confer together, so as to have a little variety in your pretenses?"

The man laughed and explained that, as no liquor could be had in the town, the only way they could get it was by buying it from vessels in the harbor, and they had found the pretense of the sickness useful in inducing visitors to violate the law by selling to them.

There was one other occurrence that Sunday morning which today might be considered unusual. All the yachtsmen came ashore and went to church.

Pew rent, incidentally, was not high in the Boothbay church in the old days. In a private account book kept many years ago by a resident of the town, I came across the following entries:

"January, 1819. Wm. Brier 2d agreed for three seats in my part of Pew No. 16 at 50 cts. per year each, in all $1.50 per year.

"January 13, 1820. Wm. Brier 2d paid me in fish

for the use of my Pew last year. 75 lbs. at 2 cts., $1.50."

The inland visitor to the Maine coast has new varieties of birds, animals, and plants presented to his view. He may know little about them and not care a great deal, but they force themselves on his notice and sooner or later, possibly through some oddity of presentation, he finds himself taking an interest in them.

The bird life around the cove could scarcely fail to attract attention, as the birds practically knock at your door or come down the chimney unannounced. The cove often echoes with the cries of both land birds and sea birds going about their avocations. Perhaps most noticeable are the cawing of the crows holding a town meeting in the pines or flying noisily across to the point for blackberries, or the piping of sea gulls hovering over the returning tide to see what it is bringing them.

A favorite resort of the gulls is a half-tide ledge on one side of the cove. Here they spend the siesta hour, the period when they are inactive, and settle down quietly on the seaweed-covered rocks which in the sunlight are a yellowish brown, in the shade a deep chocolate, and against which the adult gulls look intensely white. The young gulls in brown plumage act like fools. They peep continuously, nodding their heads at the same time, and behaving in the annoying fashion of ill-mannered juveniles.

A gull is a beautifully buoyant bird. It sits or swims in the water with its tail up at a rakish angle, like the high, sharp stern of one of the old pinkys. A duck does not hold its tail so high, consequently you can tell the difference between a duck and a gull a long way off.

Sea gulls are notoriously great scavengers and play a part in keeping the coast clean the year round, even extending the service to the land, sometimes for some distance from the sea, especially when it is stormy outside. They are sharp-eyed birds. I have seen a gull swoop down hundreds of feet to investigate a bone left by a dog on a lawn near a house. They are, of course, helpful to fishermen in detecting schools of fish. It is a beautiful sight to see hundreds of these white birds on a sunny day flying excitedly over water seething with fish.

It is possible to make pets of sea gulls. I have known children who have climbed up the rocks and taken them when young from their nests and domesticated them with the chickens, which they always dominate. A sea gull will fight the rooster of a flock and lick it. A greedy bird, it will eat out of your hand, but it always snatches and it can wound quite badly. The upper part of a gull's beak has razor edges. It can cut your finger to the bone, or make two gashes across your hand. When gulls fight they try to strike first with their wings, and the way to catch them is by their long flight feathers. A sea gull seldom has any affection for the person who tries to make a pet of it.

In the early evening blue herons come to the cove to fish, wading in stately fashion along the margin. They are rangy birds. When they arrive just after sunset their neck feathers are dry and white, but as soon as they start fishing they become wet and gray. They wade slowly and warily, their long legs going out behind them like a person walking on glassy ice. They do not disturb the water at all, making rings only when they strike. Before lunging for a fish a heron leans forward, draws in its neck in a way suggestive of a snake coiling to attack, and strikes quickly. Following each catch it shakes its head to get rid of the water, and after gulping down the fish it apparently rinses its mouth. One evening I watched a heron fishing in the rain. It struck thirty-five times in the course of two hours, and each time succeeded in getting a tiny fish or some other form of marine life. It was practically dark when it finally rose and, trailing its legs behind, flew slowly across the cove to disappear in the shadows on the other side. October twelfth is the latest I have known a heron to fish in the cove.

Across the cove there is a fish hawk's nest, a faggoty affair that doubtless smells fishy, as such nests usually do. It is occupied season after season, possibly by the same pair. The birds sail high above the water, sometimes remaining poised almost motionless for what seems an impossible length of time; but when they spot a fish in the water they drop like a sounding lead. The descent is made in two sections. Halfway down they break their plunge by flapping their wings for an instant, and then, if the fish is still there, they continue their dive. When necessary they go completely under water. They are not successful every time, but more often than not they come up with a small fish wriggling in their talons. Sometimes they seem to have difficulty holding their catch, but the prey seldom gets away.

The kingbirds which perch on the topmost branches of trees and other vantage points on the lookout for insects sometimes go after the fish hawks. They are neat, efficient birds, make little or no noise, and are splendid aerial fighters. They like to use snakeskins in their nests. In a contest with the hawks they always rout the larger birds.

But a fish hawk that will turn tail from a kingbird is not afraid of an eagle. There are eagles in Maine and once or twice during the summer one is to be seen soaring in the sky high above the cove. I have not myself ever seen hawks in the act of worrying an eagle, but one of my neighbors has, and he said the eagle appeared to turn over on its back in the air and claw at its tormentors.

Cormorants or shags, which are plentiful in neighboring waters, occasionally visit the cove. They seem to increase as the fish increase. These large birds, as black as crows, with curved red beaks and green eyes, have an evil, blackmailing look. One caught in a net at West Southport stood three feet high and had a wingspread of four feet. It bit the fisherman who captured it. I watched one which came into the cove one morning. It may have been attracted by the gulls which were crying around a fisherman busy in his dory. It gained altitude against the wind and then planed down clear across the cove in a long, fast line of flight that terminated in the water. Just before it lighted it braked itself with its wings, flapping them a few times, and then settled down easily into the water, leaving a wake not more than a yard long.

Some land birds seem out of place near the sea. Crows apparently like the coast and you even see them on the islands, but they are not equipped for water or ooze, and their presence somehow strikes one as being anachronistic. A rowdy gang of ten or a dozen haunt the cove. Sometimes they act as if they thought they were sea gulls, though they are as different from those birds as night from day, or mourning from rejoicing. They are slow flyers and in crossing the cove the oarage of their wings seems less effective than that of almost any other bird. If you happen to see three of them flying together and repeat three times the words "Three crows good luck," without seeing any others while you say it, your luck, it is alleged, will take a favorable turn.

Robins also strike one as being more of an inland type of bird, while swallows seem to be at home by the sea. In the early evening they frequently hawk insects close to the water, sometimes flying so close as to touch it lightly. When Napoleon Bonaparte Fickett was keeper of Pond Island Light at the mouth of the Kennebec River, he used to leave the doors of the boathouse open in early spring in readiness for the swallows that made it their home every year. And all the year round the gulls used to come up to the back door of the keeper's house to be fed.

The cove has its quota of nocturnal birds. I have been awakened in the dead of night by the harsh, raucous clamor of a night heron, and I have been startled by an owl flying silently past me in the darkness. I have agreeable recollections of the whippoorwills calling to one another in the evening, when the fireflies were busy and the waters of the cove reflected the stars.

Flowers thrive around the cove, not only the cultivated kind, but the wild variety as well, and the sea air works wonders with them, intensifying

their colors to a remarkable degree. Along the
shore in July, amid bayberry and creeping juniper,
are such things as sea lavender, wild roses, very
pale pink primroses, paler than the roses, fireweed,
purple vetch, and thistles almost the same color as
the vetch. Purple vetch is sometimes called wild
pea. It has a small seed pod containing tiny peas,
like the garden pea pod, and in late summer,
when dry, the peas rattle in the pods as you walk
through them. The sea lavender grows closest to
the water.

There are, of course, many other plants besides
these in July, and some have already come and
gone, while others have yet to arrive. Often when
I have seen some wild flower I did not know and
have asked someone what it was, I have been put
off with, "Oh, it's just some wild thing." There is
something curiously careless and Philistine in that
vague answer.

Lilies prosper in Maine. Even beside the sea they
are tough-stalked enough to withstand the wind.
Moose like to eat the shoots of water lilies. When
Thoreau visited the state in 1857 he collected some
bulbs of the wild yellow lily *(Lilium canadense)*
for a soup. His Indian guide, Joe Polis, had told him
that his people used the bulbs for this purpose, and
Thoreau turned chef in the woods.

"Following the Indian's directions," he said, "I
washed the bulbs carefully, minced some moose-

meat and some pork, salted and boiled all together, but we had not patience to try the experiment fairly, for he said it must be boiled till the roots were completely softened so as to thicken the soup like flour; but though we left it on all night, we found it dried to the kettle in the morning, and not yet boiled to a flour. Perhaps the roots were not ripe enough, for they commonly gather them in the fall."

The woods bordering on the cove are like a drugstore stocked with old-fashioned remedies. Goldthread grows on the shady point on the easterly side. This little evergreen has a perennial creeping root, which is a bright orange-yellow, and it is this color that gives the plant its name. The root is intensely bitter and was once much used in New England as a local application for canker.

Snakeroot presumably got its name from its supposed power to offset the bite of a rattlesnake, but in domestic practice it was originally employed in rheumatism. The root was the part used; a piece of it was boiled for a short time in a pint of water. It was administered in tea and used in conjunction with slippery elm before childbirth, as it was supposed to assist nature in such cases.

Juniper berries were also believed to be efficacious in the cure of wounds caused by the bite of poisonous snakes. Eating eight or ten berries in the morning was considered good for a bad cough.

They were thought to be a great resistor of pestilence. They are still used in the preparation of gin, and that is how most people like to take juniper berries today.

Fir balsam was thought to be good for sore nipples, fresh wounds, and weakness of the stomach. Then there are balm of Gilead, witch hazel, and many more. Within a short distance of the cove is the site of the ancient Indian herb garden on Indiantown Island.

It is always an event of great interest when a school of fish comes into the cove. Sometimes the fish are small herring three or four inches long, sometimes small mackerel, either tinkers or smaller. A fisherman told me he called the smallest mackerel thole pins. None of the schools that comes in is large. Four or five hundred bushels is about the limit, but that is not a bad catch at a dollar or so a bushel. It is when you see the inner end of the cove alive with fish and the net being run across from shore to shore that you realize what a natural fish trap the place is, and this is true of innumerable other coves up and down the coast.

The only fisherman living at the cove is Alden Swett, who is one of the best fishermen in the Boothbay region. He gets all the fish that enter the cove, but he does not wait for them to come—he goes out after them, and his biggest catches are made elsewhere. Three thousand bushels is a good catch, but a thousand is by no means unsatisfactory. Once when he made a small catch of a few hundred bushels near Sawyer's Island he had to leave them for several days. "The seals and the gulls got most of them," he said.

It requires a good deal of equipment for fishing on this scale. In addition to his boats and other gear, Alden Swett has three hundred fathoms of net, which during the season has to be pickled every day and overhauled about every two weeks. If it were not for the daily sousing of the net with salt water, it would rot and fall to pieces when picked up.

Besides being on the lookout for herring and mackerel, Alden Swett usually has out about a hundred and twenty-five lobster traps, which is enough to keep most men fully occupied.

Every house on the cove has its well, though during the summer everybody uses the town water supply, which is available through surface pipes. This summer water comes from a large pond which one season became such a popular place of resort for sea gulls that the town had to hire a boy to sit in a boat all day to scare them away. The water is excellent, but the natives as a rule prefer to drink well water. Carpenters engaged in building a garage at one of the houses on the cove used to send one of their number some distance to a well for water. Thinking to save them this trouble, I told them to help themselves to my town supply, but they declined. They said the old well they were drawing from was a particularly fine one. It was like drinking glacier water.

"It's nonsense," one of them told me, "to have the water in your well analyzed. Either it is drinkable, or it isn't. If it's drinkable, it's all right."

During dry spells of weather there is apt to be a lot of talk about wells. The man who has one that hasn't failed his family for generations is proud of it. Whenever a new well is dug there is always the keenest interest to know how far it was necessary to go to strike water. In some places the hazel stick is still used to locate the likeliest place for a well. In the hands of an experienced dowser, this ancient method of finding water apparently works like magic.

One frequently sees fine granite wellheads in Maine. A cove resident who has a wooden cover over his old well keeps it padlocked in summer when his grandchildren come to visit, as he does not want them playing around the well and perhaps falling into it. Plenty of New Englanders have lost their lives in wells—well-diggers by the earth's caving in on them, and children and others by accidentally tumbling down them. The cove well just mentioned is piped into the house for winter use. In extremely cold weather the old custom is followed of hanging a lighted lantern down the well to keep it from freezing.

The rise and fall of the tide in the cove is about ten feet, but it is too steep-sided a place for extensive flats to be uncovered at low water, and consequently there is none of the mucky, clam-flat smell which you get at places that have their shallow pretenses exposed by the ebb. Yet clams are dug at the cove, and it was probably a clam digger who unearthed the remarkably fine Indian ax which was picked up on the shore between high- and low-water mark.

The place is rich in Indian relics. Bone fishhooks have been found and jasper arrowheads and other artifacts. The arrowheads were something of a mystery, as there is no jasper in the area. But they may have come from the jasper cave on the New Hampshire line, which was largely made by the Indians chipping away the stone for arrowheads, perhaps over a period of centuries.

If it were possible to choose the time of day when high tide would be most welcome at the cove, I should cast my ballot for the middle of the morning, as there are not many shadows then and the cove is apt to be less interesting than at other times. It would help to have it full of sea water.

There is, of course, a difference between shadow and reflection, and there are days when the cove reflects the clouds and rocks and trees and boats

so perfectly that you can see no difference between
the original and the reproduction. This occurs on
calm days when the surface of the cove is as smooth
as a mirror.

After a storm the tide often brings in a lot of
loose seaweed, and the cove looks like the Sargasso
Sea. But the wind usually drives it to one side or
the other and it soon disappears. The extra high
tides when the moon is full also bring in seaweed
and driftwood.

There is a good deal of crystallized wealth in the
rocks of Maine. Such semi-precious stones as tour-
maline, beryl, amethyst, topaz, and garnet are to
be found in different parts of the state. I know several coves where there are garnets. An ancient
legend says that the only light in Noah's Ark was
supplied by a huge red garnet. The garnets of
Maine are not so splendid as that Talmudic speci-
men, but they are among the most attractive of the
semi-precious stones. The name of the gem comes
from its resemblance to pomegranate seeds. Garnet
crystals differ from others in being unusually sym-
metrical. Two island caves which I have visited are
studded with them—one on House Island in Muscongus Bay, the other on Pond Island, where the
lighthouse stands, at the mouth of the Kennebec
River.

From time to time there has been considerable
digging for buried treasure along the coast, but no

great store of pirate gold, silver, or precious stones has ever been discovered, though there are legends of such lucky finds. Occasionally a modest crock of cash has been accidentally unearthed, but even though the dates on some of this coinage go back to piratical times, its relatively small value and the absence of plate and jewelry indicates it belonged to some early settler. It is not surprising that there should have been much seeking for treasure trove in Maine, as the romantic coves and inlets of the coast have the glamour of pirate hangouts.

TO FISH THE LAKE, THE STREAM, AND THE DEEP SEA

FISHING is one of the oldest pursuits known to man. Long before there were any settlements in New England, the coastal waters of Maine were visited by Spanish, English, French, Dutch, and Portuguese fishermen, who took immense quantities of fish, principally cod. These they dried ashore, both on the mainland and on the islands, and then loaded them aboard their vessels to take back to Europe. The courage and enterprise of these men in crossing the Atlantic in their ten- and twenty-ton ships is still something at which to marvel.

In the month of April, 1614, Captain John Smith with two ships from London arrived at Monhegan Island. His plan was to capture whales and make "tryalls of a Myne of Gold or Copper." If these failed, fish and furs were to be his resource. Although the Indians in their speedy birch canoes were able to surround and kill a whale, Captain Smith and his men in their heavier and slower boats did not succeed. "We saw many; spent much time in chasing them; but did not kill any." After "long lingering about the whale," they finally got down to the business of fishing, and in the space of a few months caught and cured enough fish to make a handsome profit on their North American voyage.

All the early adventurers were enthusiastic about Maine, which they saw as a land of magnificent harbors, rivers, and forests. "A high country, full of great woods and goodly groves, and sundry sort of beasts; whose waters teemed with sea fowl, plenty of salmon, lobsters, and other fishes of great bigness." It is related that in 1607 there was such a great store of lobsters along the coast that you could lade a ship with them. One boat's crew killed fifty large ones near an island in an hour. This was at low water and the lobsters could be seen on the bottom not more than half a fathom deep. The crew hitched them up with an improvised gaff made with a big hook fastened to the end of a staff. Some of these lobsters weighed twenty pounds or more.

The present-day fisherman, of course, does not ordinarily get such whacking specimens. A lobster has little chance nowadays of surviving long enough to attain great size. Even if a fisherman did land a big one, he would be obliged to throw it back. Maine has a double-gauge lobster law. No lobster can be taken or sold whose body shell measures less than three and one-eighth inches or more than five inches in length. Egg-bearing females cannot be taken at all, unless wanted by the state for rearing purposes. They are marked with a V on the middle flipper of the tail.

A female lobster produces from three to five thousand eggs every other year, but when hatched under natural conditions very few live to become adult lobsters. It is believed by some authorities that not more than four or five out of each spawning mature. The eggs form inside the lobster, but are presently expelled, and adhere to a sticky substance on the body shell under the tail. Here they remain until hatched. This takes from nine to eleven months, depending on the temperature of the water. When at length hatching takes place the tiny organisms come to the surface, where they are the sport of winds and waves and tides, which take a heavy toll of them by washing them ashore. Other fishes eat them, and they also eat one another. Only a small minority reach the fourth stage of life, when they are able to sink to the bottom and find comparative safety from the perils that beset them when helplessly adrift on the surface. By this time they have grown to be half an inch or so long and look like full-grown lobsters. It takes five years for a lobster to reach legal size.

Because of the fame and popularity of Maine lobsters, artificial propagation is necessary to maintain the supply. On Juniper Point in Boothbay Harbor the state maintains a lobster-rearing station with a capacity of six million baby lobsters a year. When females are needed for rearing purposes the state buys egg-bearers from the fishermen who find them in their traps. These lobsters are placed in "pounds" until they are ready to hatch, when they are taken to the rearing station. The young lobsters are raised on a diet of finely ground liver until they reach the bottom-seeking stage. This takes fifteen or sixteen days during which time they shed their shells and grow new ones three times. A baby lobster sheds seventeen times its first year, but afterward only once annually. During the rearing process they are kept in tanks through which salt water is continuously pumped, the swirling stream keeping them so busy that they are unable to indulge in the vice of cannibalism. At this stage of their careers they are placed in cans and are released at various places along the coast. A fair number of these attain edible size and eventually reach our tables.

Although Maine people have always appreciated the superb quality of the native lobster as an article of food, it was not until supplies of the crustacean became depleted elsewhere that the demand for Maine lobsters became widespread and began to assume its present proportions. In 1880 the landed value of the lobster fishery was only half a million dollars, whereas today it is worth from six to eight millions, and is the most important of Maine's shellfish industries. The largest catch was made in 1946, when a total of nineteen million pounds were landed. That year there were over six thousand licensed lobster fishermen working nearly half a million traps and operating upwards of four thousand motorboats and a host of lesser craft. This lobster navy, and the traps and gear used, represented an investment of millions.

Modern means of transportation have helped to spread the fame of Maine lobsters and build up the fishery. By the use of air express, railway express, and other fast carrier services, lobsters can be delivered fresh to all parts of the United States. Improved methods of handling, packing, and refrigeration have enhanced the quality of lobsters sent to distant places and have also served to cut down the high death rate, which has been the cause of the wide discrepancy between what the fisherman gets for a lobster and what it brings in the retail market. Many lobsters die while captive in the pounds as well as during shipment.

These storage pounds in which the lobsters are kept while awaiting shipment are situated at convenient places along the coast from Casco Bay to Eastport. There are about fifty of them from which a steady flow of lobsters is maintained to markets near and far. Thus a spell of bad weather, when perhaps for days the fisherman cannot get out to tend their traps, does not cut off the supply. The lobster dealers who have the pounds send out lobster smacks with wells to collect lobsters from fishermen in the small coves and harbors along the mainland and out among the islands. Pending the arrival of the smacks, the fisherman keeps his lobsters in a submerged wooden cage called a car. Often this is a raft with a shanty built on top and the enclosure for the lobsters underneath. The captive lobsters have to be fed. Some fishermen save the crabs which they find in their lobster pots for this purpose.

One of the largest lobsters taken on the Maine coast in modern times was a thirty-six-pounder fished up out of the waters of Casco Bay. Once in a blue moon a blue lobster is caught. The one I saw had a translucent shell that was as blue as old-fashioned china. It was locally believed to be poisonous, perhaps because there is a nautical prejudice against blue. To paint anything blue on a vessel is supposed to be bad luck.

Among lobstermen, the fisherman who does not play the game and who makes a practice of taking undersize lobsters, called shorts, is looked upon with disapproval, since if they all did it the fishery would be ruined in the course of time. Fishermen have a way of settling their own disputes. If one of them persists in violating local fishing customs, he is likely to find his traps cut loose, with little chance of finding them. Even though he makes them himself, it costs a fisherman about three dollars to build a trap.

Storms often play havoc with the lobster fisherman's equipment. A dozen traps may be washed away and destroyed in a single night. The number of fathoms of line on a trap must be more than enough to reach from the surface buoy to the bottom, because if there is no slack to play about in heavy weather, the trap is dragged and damaged or destroyed. To keep the slack from chafing on the rocks below, some fishermen attach a corked bottle or small buoy to the line several fathoms from the trap. Each fisherman paints his surface buoys a distinctive color to distinguish them from those of other lobstermen.

A fisherman with, say, a hundred and twenty-five traps distributes them in various places, perhaps a dozen or fifteen near an island, another group close to a ledge, and possibly a line of them along the rocky shore of a headland. The traps are set by compass bearings, so the fisherman knows the course to run in thick weather. In winter when the lobsters seek deeper water to get away from the cold, the fisherman moves his traps out too. From about the middle of February to the first of April lobsters lie buried in the mud, and the lobsterman brings his gear ashore for overhauling. Pot buoys are repainted, the twine heads of the traps mended and tarred, other repairs are made, and new traps built. There is never any resting on the oars for the lobster fisherman. Out on the water in all kinds of weather, the life of a lobsterman has its hardships and dangers, but he is his own boss and values his independence.

Several species of shellfish found on the Maine coast are rarely eaten there, but they are liked in other parts of the country, and consequently local fishermen pay some attention to them. There is only a limited market for sea urchins, mussels, and periwinkles, as most people are unfamiliar with these seafoods and are chary of buying them.

Once I asked a Maine man if he had ever eaten any sea urchins. "No," he said emphatically. "The stuff that comes out of them is like stepping on a caterpillar."

The urchin, however, is highly esteemed as an article of food by some people, particularly

Italians, and the Fulton Fish Market in New York handles many Maine sea urchins. The Chinese are also said to be fond of the orange-red roe, which is the only edible part of these curious marine creatures. Each urchin yields several teaspoonfuls of roe.

Maine is not much of a place for shells, as they are ground to pieces by the rocks, but there are stretches of beach where it is very usual to find those of sea urchins. One of the most interesting beaches in Maine is on Metinic Island, which is seldom visited except by fishermen. Walking along this beach early one spring I saw many urchin shells which had been washed up by the winter storms. The shell is globular and spiny and measures some three inches across. It has a hole in one side and looks something like a doughnut.

Extreme care has to be exercised in taking a sea urchin from its native haunts. The prickly spines which serve for defense and locomotion are as sharp as needles and can remain in your skin as obstinately as a splinter. One would almost as willingly encounter an affectionate porcupine. The sea urchin is often appropriately called the hedgehog of the sea. Another name for it is sea chestnut, obviously derived from the fact that its exterior is like that of a prickly chestnut bur. Less politely, it is also known as a whore's egg. And science has outdone itself by labeling it *Strongylocentrotus.*

A Maine fisherman I know who goes after sea urchins always gathers them at low tide. He finds them along the coast and up the tidal rivers. He said they are more difficult to get in rough weather than in calm weather, as they cling to the rocks harder when it is rough and relax when it is calm. His best haul was thirty-five bushels in three hours, for which he received a dollar a bushel. They are shipped to market in barrels, and retail for about fifty cents a dozen. Some people like the roe better than caviar.

Practically all mussels taken by Maine fishermen are canned. Although between two and three million pounds are packed yearly, one hears little about this fishery, because Eastern people as a rule do not eat this shellfish. The leading market for the Maine product is the West Coast.

The giant sea scallops which once abounded along the coast, especially in Penobscot Bay, have decreased so rapidly in recent years that fears are felt that this once important fishery may altogether vanish. During the past thirty-five years the catch has dwindled from over two million pounds to about one hundred thousand pounds. Veteran scallop draggers believe starfish are responsible for the decline.

That the Indians were fond of shellfish we know from the great accumulations of shells which they left at their favorite places of resort. They visited the seacoast in summer to feast on fishes and to cure supplies of seafood for winter consumption. As is well known, the largest of these shell heaps, which are found all along the coast, are at Damariscotta. At Indiantown Island, near Southport, Dexter Hodgdon of Boothbay Harbor has found many redskin relics in the shell banks. The best time to look for them is after storms and spring tides, he told me. Several Indian skeletons have been discovered here in good condition, the shells apparently possessing some preservative quality. One noticeable thing about all these aboriginal banqueting sites is that the Indians knew how to choose good locations for their summer encampments.

Most of the shells found in the ancient Indian deposits are clam shells. Oyster shells have also been found, which has led some people to believe that oysters once thrived in great numbers in the inshore waters, but died off from some unknown cause. Oysters still grow in a few places, but not in commercial quantities, and experiments hold out little hope of establishing an oyster fishery.

Next to lobstering, the clam fishery is the most important of Maine's shellfish industries. In 1948 some thirty-three hundred licensed clam diggers produced nearly ten million pounds and received over two million dollars for their work. Some of the clams are sold fresh, but most of them find their way to the clam factories, where they are canned or made into broth or chowder.

Digging clams with a short-handled clam hoe is back-breaking work, but many families in certain coastal areas are dependent on the clam fishery for a living. It is a common sight to see the bent figures of the clammers as they tap along the mud flats at low tide. When the clams, disturbed by the tapping, give away their hiding places by spouting tiny jets of water, they are dug out of the mud. Clamming is not just a matter of getting out on the flats and working until the returning tide makes it impossible to remain longer. Clams can be sold by the bushel unshucked, but "shocking" and selling them to the clam factories by the gallon pays better, and many families, young and old alike, work at getting the freshly harvested clams out of their shells. Quite young girls who can dig a bushel on a tide will spend the rest of the day helping their families with the shucking. After each clamming tide, thick blue smoke from the fires over which the soft-shelled bivalves are steamed rises from the homes of the clam diggers. It's not an enviable life. I have seen the clammers at work in the vicinity of Jonesport in cold weather, when the world was stiff with frost and searching winds swept the flats. But the diggers are a hardy race.

Although many of the clam flats have been partly exhausted, through intensive harvesting, a more or less steady flow of clams into the canneries has been maintained. The sardine canneries, on the other hand, are dependent on the fish's running. If there are no herring to process, the factories close down, and the community suffers. When a catch is landed the whistle or siren is blown calling in the workers, who are mostly women and girls, and you see them streaming toward the factory.

The business of canning sardines began at Eastport in 1875, and the eastern end of the coast is still the center of the industry, with the largest factories at Lubec, three miles across the bay from Eastport. Lubec is one of the most picturesque and fishiest-smelling towns in Maine. It used to be said that the odor of the sardine canneries wafted across the water to the near-by Canadian island of Campobello spoiled that place as a summer resort.

The American sardine, of course, is just a youthful herring, and when first packed in Maine it was labeled to make people think it was a genuine French sardine. Southern members of Congress, when asked to protect the industry, used to wax pretty sarcastic about the practice of using French trade-marks, even though the cottonseed oil in which the fish were packed came from the south. It is doubtful, however, if anyone was really fooled by the fake French labels.

Long before the herring began to be canned in Maine they were smoked and many are still put up in this way. They are also kippered, salted dry, pickled, and ground up for cocktail paste. Processors also use them in fertilizer, in fish meals, and in various fish oils. An important use is for lobster bait. Even the scales, which were once considered worthless, are made into an essence used in manufacturing artificial pearls. The herring is the jack-of-all-trades among Maine coast fishes.

It is not surprising that the Eastport-Lubec salient should be the headquarters of the herring trade, because, while these fish are to be found the whole length of the coast, nowhere are they normally present in such numbers as in Passamaquoddy Bay. On a dark night a large school of herring will light up a cove. The early way of catching them was to run them into an inlet or natural trap in the coast. Later, artificial fish traps or weirs made of brush or netting were used. They were strategically placed so that the schools would enter them when they came in with the tide. Now seines, which are large nets with sinkers on one edge and floats on the other, are generally used to surround them. The sardine pack in Maine runs to about three million cases annually.

A distant relative of the herring is the alewife, which, like the shad and salmon, comes up the rivers in the spring to spawn. Great numbers are taken, some of which are smoked for local consumption, but most are salted in barrels for export.

One day late in May on the Damariscotta River road below Newcastle I gave a man a lift who was carrying a stick of alewives smoked to a deep tobacco brown. He said he had gotten them from a man named Harrington who caught them in a cove. He explained that formerly there were weirs along the river in which the alewives were trapped.

"They don't sell so well as they did," he continued. "Some people don't like them, but they are good eating."

A famous alewife stream in this same locality extends along the borders of the towns of Damariscotta Mills and Nobleborough. It is a short, shallow stream which for a few days every spring boils with a myriad of alewives striving to reach the spawning ponds at its head. There is great activity along its banks at this season, as men with long-handled nets take hundreds of thousands of alewives from its waters. By no means all the fish that come here are caught. Only half are taken, and the other half are not molested. It all depends on the route the fish take. The stream has two mouths and by an agreement between the two towns dating back more than a century, the fish which enter what is called the Sacred Stream are permitted to pass unhindered to the spawning grounds, while those which take the other way are doomed. To be or not to be—that is the question for the fish, with the outcome depending on the route taken. The towns share equally in the fishing rights of the stream, which they **lease** to commercial fishing interests, and split the profit. This self-imposed conservation measure has worked well, and the spring phenomenon of the alewife run continues to be an annual fixture.

There are fashions in fish as well as in other things. Cod fishermen once had no use for haddock and tossed them back into the ocean. But along in the seventies a remarkable change in the popular taste took place. Finnan haddie became the rage, and fresh haddock supplanted the cod in popular favor. Fifteen years ago the rosefish, bream, redfish, or sea perch was considered a waste species, but today it leads all other fish in value, including the herring, to which it stands second, however, in point of production. Rosefish fillets are extremely popular in the Middle West. It is the changing fashion in fish—the use of a variety like rosefish—which has enabled Maine to maintain its annual yield in the face of declining supplies of such species as cod, haddock, hake, pollock, cusk, and halibut.

Salt-water sport fishing is a leading summer pastime in Maine, the coastal waters offering a variety of fish. The deep-sea varieties taken include cod, cusk, hake, and halibut. Fly-casting for mackerel and pollock attracts many people, as both are gamey fish, especially the pollock. Trolling offshore for giant tuna or horse mackerel draws many rod-and-reel sportsmen. The commercial tuna fishermen use

the less thrilling but surer method of harpooning
the fish. There is some surf fishing for striped sea
bass.

There is a curious Maine business connected
with salt-water sports fishing: the worm trade—
not the garden variety of worm, but marine
worms, bloodworms, and sandworms, which are
dug on the coast for use as live bait for dock and
surf fishing. These worms are sold all along the
eastern seaboard, but the chief markets for them
are New York and Philadelphia, where they are
in great demand during the summer months,
bringing as high as five or six cents apiece. The
worms are delicate creatures and the diggers
handle them gently. Packed in very fine seaweed,
they are shipped in small market baskets, two hundred and fifty to three hundred worms to a basket.
Pending shipment they are kept in damp cellars.
The marine worm diggers turn up thousands of
them.

Fishing in Maine's inland waters provides sport
for a host of resident and nonresident anglers.
With its thousands of lakes, ponds, streams, and
brooks, Maine is natural fishing country. Despite
the growing army of persons who fish these waters
and the consequent drain on the supply of fish,
there is still good sport to be had here. It is not,
however, what it used to be in the days when many
fishing places could be reached only by canoe or on

foot over rough trails. Planes and jeeps have in recent years opened up a lot of hitherto untouched fishing territory.

Maine is essentially a trout country. The mysterious landlocked salmon, which is a subspecies of the Atlantic salmon, was found originally only in Sebago, Green, and Sebec Lakes. Propagated by the state, it has flourished, until now it shares many lakes with the native eastern brook trout, sometimes called in Maine the squaretail trout. At Wilson's East Outlet Camps on Moosehead Lake, Bill Geagan, outdoors editor of the *Bangor Daily Commercial*, recently studied old records of trout that were caught in the lake before salmon were introduced. These records were outline drawings on paper of fish weighing more than ten pounds. He believes that a few weighed nearly thirteen pounds. The big lake was then alive with trout, as were all other Maine lakes, ponds, and streams suited to them.

At that time Aroostook County, which is now the best trout region in Maine, was a paradise for the trout fisherman. Roads were few and poor, automobiles scarce and undependable. All travel to the region was by train, and to the waters by trail or canoe. The numerous lakes, ponds, streams, and brooks abounded with trout of all sizes, many of them whoppers. It was not necessary to travel far from the trails to enjoy fast fishing, so many of the

more remote waters in this vast area remained unfished for years. Nevertheless, the kill was great,
as the bag limits were generous, the fish and game
laws weak and laxly enforced.

The army of anglers grows steadily. Fast trains,
more and more highways and roads, automobiles,
and motorboats, and now planes make it relatively
easy to invade all parts of the trout country. This
has increased the pressure on the fish supply to
such an extent that in many of the popular trouting waters natural reproduction cannot keep pace
with the kill. But the state has met the situation by
heavy stocking.

Maine operates several dozen fish hatcheries and
is building more. Millions of fish are released
yearly, a large percentage of which are held in
rearing pools until they reach legal size. Stocking
has been speeded up by employing planes, fish tank
trucks, boats, and other means of distribution. Native brook trout, brown trout, and a few rainbows
are reared in the hatcheries. Landlocked salmon
and togue or lake trout are also raised in great
numbers.

The heavy fishing is not solely responsible for
the reduction of Maine's fish supply. The felling or
burning of the forests along the banks has ruined
some streams. Without the trees to retain the rainfall, it runs off in flash floods that pass quickly,
leaving the streams shallow and warm. Droughts

dry up the brooks and this spells death for a lot of trout. Pollution, especially by sawdust from lumbering and pulp operations, has had deleterious effects on the fishing in many streams. Dams do no good.

New trout waters, however, are being added by seining out of certain spring-fed ponds all rough fishes, such as perch, bass, pickerel, suckers, etc., and stocking with trout. The brown trout are found mostly in the deep lakes, and for a while in spring and summer they are taken by trolling on top, later down deep with heavy gear. They run up to fifteen pounds. And togue or lake trout, which are also very common in Maine, reach a great size.

Moosehead and nearly all the old trout waters still offer good sport. There are many distant and secluded ponds, seldom visited by man, that abound with trout. Some of these ponds are fortunately too small for planes to land on or take off from. The fish in these backwoods waters are mostly wild natives.

The vast Rangeley region is also very good trout country, with both wild fishes and others raised in hatcheries. It is interesting to glance back at the old records for this locality. A memorandum of seventy years ago of fly-fishing for brook trout in Rangeley Lake between October second and ninth shows a catch of sixty-three which averaged over four and three-quarters pounds. The largest weighed ten pounds, two others nine pounds each, two eight pounds, and none less than three pounds.

There are not many large wading streams in Maine, but it is densely dotted with trout ponds and laced with countless little brooks where trout are found in good numbers by worm fishermen.

TO RELISH LOBSTERS AND
BLUEBERRY PIE

LOBSTER stands at the top of Maine's marine bill of fare. The clear, cold waters of the coast are extremely favorable to this shellfish. Fish instinctively seek the places where the food and the temperature of the water suit them best, and it is in these places that they are at their prime. Save for the period during the summer when they shed their shells, Maine lobsters are unsurpassable. A shedder is soft and flabby and not good eating, but as the lobsters dwelling along the coast begin to shed before those living up the salt rivers, the supply of edible lobsters is pretty constant.

The Indians broiled their lobsters and used the big claws for pipes. It was easier for them to broil lobsters than to boil them, because originally they had no kettles, and their method of broiling was the slow one of dropping hot stones into a clay-covered basket filled with water. But a lobster is better broiled than boiled, and the Indians probably recognized its superior flavor when cooked in this way. Oddly enough, white people for centuries preferred to drop a lobster into a pot of boiling water, but gradually there has been a return to the Indian method, and broiled live lobster is now the classic way to eat the crustacean.

Splitting, cleaning, and broiling a lobster is simple. Most cook books give only one way of splitting, and that is to lay the lobster on its back, make a deep incision at the mouth with a sharp, strong knife, and draw the blade quickly through the entire length of the body and tail. But the method I have seen used, and have used many times myself, is to place the lobster on its back on a board, and then holding the sharp edge of a long knife lengthwise of the creature's body, give the back of the knife a tap or two with a hammer, thus cleaving the lobster from stem to stern almost down to the shell. Whichever method is used, the large claws should be cracked with a hammer or mallet, or a nutcracker should be provided when lobsters are served.

After splitting the lobster, it should be opened flat and the "sand vein," the "crop" or "craw," and the stomach removed. These are easily recognizable. The small "sand vein" or intestinal canal extends through the middle of the body to the tail. Often but not always it is a darker color than the meat. The "crop" or "craw" is a small sac close to the mouth, and the stomach is also near the head end. The bright orange substance found in some lobsters is the "coral," and is considered a great delicacy. It occurs only in lady lobsters. It is their ovaries. If you like "coral," buy female lobsters, which are distinguished from the males by the greater breadth of their tails.

After you have brushed the meat with melted butter, the lobster is ready to broil. Whether you broil it over an open fire in an indoor or outdoor fireplace or under the flame in the broiler of a stove, place the lobster back down, and broil about ten minutes on each side or until the meat is done. People addicted to broiling lobsters over open fires know that a very hot bed of coals is necessary. The advantage of the open-fire method is that if you have a large enough grate you can broil eight or ten lobsters at a time. For this kind of work you need a couple of long-handled forks for turning the lobsters. Lobsters weighing a pound and a half or two pounds are best.

The official State of Maine recipe for broiled lobster calls for a dressing to be spread in the cavity from which the stomach has been removed. This consists of 1½ cups of cracker crumbs or cracker meal and ½ teaspoon of salt, moistened with 2 tablespoons of Worcestershire sauce and 4 tablespoons of melted butter. After this dressing has been generously spread in the cavity, the small claws of each lobster are cut off and pressed into the dressing, four on a side, like oars. The lobster is then placed on a buttered broiler and broiled 8 to 10 minutes on the flesh side, and then turned and broiled 6 to 8 minutes on the shell side. It is served with melted butter, one lobster to each person.

Some people consider lobster baked in seaweed to be equal to, if not better than, one that has been broiled. It is the picnic way of preparing it. My experience with these bakes is confined to those given by the late Dr. Charles Moulton of New Harbor, who was a native of Maine and a master at lobster baking. He gave the bakes on the rocky shore before his house. There was a good deal of work involved, as quantities of driftwood had to be collected and a mass of seaweed pulled. The fire, which was started long in advance, was built in a cleft in the rocks across which a large sheet of iron was placed. When the rocks and the iron were thoroughly heated, a thick layer of seaweed was placed on the sheet of iron above the fire, and the lobsters, unsplit, were arranged on this bed. They were then covered with a layer of seaweed, on which corn and potatoes were placed, and on these more seaweed was piled. Occasionally during the cooking the steaming seaweed was wet down with salt water to keep it from drying out over the hot driftwood fire. At the end of an hour the lobsters and the corn and potatoes were done. The potatoes, I thought, were apt to be soggy, so instead I ate a second lobster.

It takes long practice to make a good lobster stew. Very few persons know the art of making a perfect one. The standard recipe is fairly simple and not difficult to follow, but to create a lobster stew that is a genuine work of art takes a gifted person. Here is Maine's award-winning recipe.

LOBSTER STEW

Boil a 1½ pound lobster and remove the meat immediately, saving also the tomalley or liver, the coral, and the thick white substance, or blood, from inside the shell. Simmer the tomalley and coral in ½ cup butter or margarine 7 or 8 minutes. Use a very heavy kettle. Then add the lobster meat, cut into fairly large pieces. Cook all together 10 minutes over low heat. Remove from heat, or push kettle back on stove, and cool slightly. Then add, very slowly, 1 quart rich milk, stirring constantly. Allow the stew to stand 5 or 6 hours before reheating for serving. This is one of the secrets of truly fine flavor. You do not need salt or pepper when stew is prepared in this manner. Serves 4.

The success of this stew depends largely on the stirring. If not stirred properly it will curdle. Experts declare that the outcome is contingent on the partial cooling before the milk is added, which must be done slowly and gently almost drop by drop; the continuous stirring until the stew turns to a rich yellowish red; and lastly, the "aging," which improves the flavor. Opinions differ on this final point, but Maine's premier stew-makers insist that it stand for two days. Usually five or six hours is all that is allowed.

One way to stretch lobster salad is to mix the lobster with halibut as shown in the following recipe.

LOBSTER SALAD

2 cups chopped lobster meat	1 tablespoon vinegar or lemon juice
1 cup steamed or boiled halibut	salt and pepper to taste

Pick out meat from boiled lobster while it is still warm and cut into pieces. Remove bones from halibut and while lobster and halibut are warm mix together. Add vinegar or lemon juice and season to taste. Mix well, place in covered jar and leave in refrigerator for at least 3 or 4 hours. You will find the halibut absorbs the taste and juice of the lobster and no one can tell the difference when this combination is served in a salad. Place on crisp lettuce, add your favorite salad dressing to the mixture, and decorate with olives and radishes.

Maine is rich in many other seafoods besides lobster, and the following recipes show various ways in which these other foods have been prepared for many years by Maine housewives.

FRIED CLAM CAKES

1 pint fresh clams	2 cups flour
1 teaspoon baking powder	½ teaspoon salt
	½ cup clam liquor
1 cup milk	deep fat for frying
2 eggs	

Mix the flour, baking powder, and salt and sift. Add the well-beaten eggs, milk, and clam liquor slowly to this mixture, stir well and add the clams which have been ground quite fine in a food chopper. Drop by large spoonfuls into hot, deep fat. When nicely browned, remove from kettle and drain. Serve while hot. Serves 4.

MAINE CLAM CHOWDER

1 quart clams, canned or fresh	1 onion diced or chopped
¼ pound salt pork	1 quart rich milk, scalded
1 quart diced potatoes	salt and pepper to taste
	butter, if desired

Remove black parts from clams, saving the liquor. Cut pork in small pieces and fry until crisp and golden brown, then remove small pieces of pork from the fat. Add potatoes and onion, with just enough hot water to be seen through the potatoes. Cook over low heat—just simmering—until done. If cooked over high heat, the chowder is apt to stick and burn. Finally, add clams and cook 2 minutes after bringing to a boil; longer cooking will toughen the clams.

Remove chowder from heat and let stand a few minutes, then add hot milk, the clam liquor, and seasonings to taste. By adding these last, there is less chance that the chowder will curdle, which often happens if seasonings are added before the hot milk. Add 1 tablespoon butter just before serving, or place a bit in each soup bowl. This quantity yields 6 large servings or 8 small.

Note: Like lobster stew or chowder, clam chowder should "age" a few hours, to be at its best. The flavor is always finer the second day.

CLAMBURGERS

1 pint of clams, chopped fine	1 cup cracker crumbs
	1 teaspoon salt
1 egg, well beaten	¼ teaspoon pepper

Combine ingredients in the order given and mix well. Form in round cakes and fry in hot fat, about 1 inch deep. Drain and serve piping hot.

FRIED CLAMS IN BATTER

Beat the yolks of two eggs until thick and lemon-colored. Add ½ cup milk, 1 teaspoon olive oil, 1 cup sifted bread flour, ¼ teaspoon salt, and 1 tablespoon lemon juice. Fold in 2 stiffly-beaten egg whites and add 1 pint small clams. Let stand in the refrigerator at least 2 hours. Fry in hot fat until a golden brown. Fry only a few at a time as too many cool the fat. Serves 5.

CRAB DELICIOUS

1 cup light cream
1 cup boiled rice
salt and paprika, to taste
1 cup flaked crab-meat
2 tablespoons melted butter or margarine
3 tablespoons ketchup
patty shells or toast

Heat cream and cooked rice together in top of double boiler over hot water. Season to taste, adding celery or parsley salt, if preferred to paprika. When well heated and blended, stir in the crab-meat and butter. Heat through and just before serving, stir in ketchup. Serve at once in patty shells or on crisp toast. Serves 4.

SARDINE SURPRISE

Bone 1 tin of sardines. Dry slightly on absorbent paper. Roll pie pastry one-eighth of an inch thick and cut into strips slightly wider than the length of the sardine.

Place a sardine on a strip of pastry. Sprinkle with lemon juice. Cut off enough pastry to wrap sardine and pinch edges together. Bake in a very hot oven (450° F.) for 10 to 15 minutes. Serve as an appetizer.

DEVILED SARDINES

2 cans boneless sardines	1 teaspoon Worcestershire sauce
2 tablespoons butter	½ cup fine cracker crumbs
¼ teaspoon dry mustard	1 lemon

Drain oil from sardines. Cream butter and work the mustard and Worcestershire sauce into it. Mash sardines and add to butter mixture; then add cracker crumbs. Place on clean quahog shells or in shallow baking pan and broil until golden brown. Serve hot with quarters of lemon. Serves 4.

BAKED SCALLOPS

Wash fresh scallops quickly in cold water. Drain and dry well. From each one, remove the hard piece which is on the side. Wipe carefully, roll in flour. Put in greased pan. Fill with rich milk to about ½ the depth of scallops. Dot with butter, salt, and pepper to taste. After baking about ½ hour in medium oven (350° F.), turn each and brown on other side. Do not cook in too hot an oven or the milk will curdle and be unsightly.

FRIED SCALLOPS

1 pint or 1 pound of scallops. (Maine scallops
are the deep-sea variety.) Wash scallops quickly in
cold water; drain and dry thoroughly. If they are
large, cut into cubes of about three-quarters of an
inch. Roll in seasoned flour, then in slightly beaten
egg diluted with milk or water (allow 1 tablespoon
liquid for each egg), then roll again in seasoned
flour and bread crumbs (half-and-half). Fry in
deep hot fat (375° F.) about 4 minutes or until
golden brown. Place only a single layer in a
greased frying basket, so that all will be evenly
browned. Skim fat and reheat if necessary before
cooking another layer. Drain on soft paper. Serve
with Tartar Sauce:

> 1 cup mayonnaise
> 2 tablespoons chopped pickle
>   (cucumber or sweet pickle)
> 1 tablespoon chopped olives
> 2 teaspoons minced onion
> 1 tablespoon chopped parsley

Mix sauce just before serving. The scallops will
serve 4, the sauce 6 or 8.

SCALLOPS AU GRATIN

Wash and drain 1 quart of scallops. Cover with
cold water, heat slowly to boiling, and drain. Line
a greased baking dish with a thin layer of bread
crumbs. Add scallops in layers. Sprinkle each layer

with salt, minced green pepper, and finely chopped celery until all the scallops are used. Pour over the dish 1 cup of warmed rich milk. Top with bread crumbs to which have been added 2 tablespoons grated Parmesan cheese and bake in a moderate oven (350° F.) 30 minutes. Serves 5.

SHRIMP COCKTAIL

Put 1 tablespoon of cocktail sauce in bottom of each glass. Add 3 chilled shrimp, another tablespoon sauce, then fill glass to brim with shrimp and cover with cocktail sauce. Serve with lemon wedges.

COCKTAIL SAUCE

¾ cup tomato ketchup

2-4 tablespoons fresh grated horseradish or ¼ cup prepared horseradish

10 drops Tabasco sauce

1 tablespoon Worcestershire sauce

2 tablespoons lemon juice

¼ teaspoon salt

SHRIMP AND ONION DELIGHT

12 small white onions

4½ tablespoons margarine

4½ tablespoons flour

½ teaspoon salt

dash of pepper

½ teaspoon celery salt

3 cups warm milk

2 egg yolks

2½ cups cooked shrimp

2½ cups hot mashed potatoes

½ cup grated cheese

Peel onions and cook rapidly until tender, but not falling apart. Prepare a white sauce by melting the margarine over direct heat; combine flour with seasonings and add slowly, cooking and stirring until mixture is well blended and bubbling. Gradually add the milk, stirring constantly. When smooth and thickened, remove from heat and add a little of the hot sauce to the slightly beaten egg yolks. Combine the two mixtures, stir well, then return to low heat and cook 2 minutes.

Add shrimp and drained onions and turn into a greased heat-resistant serving dish. Arrange a narrow border of hot mashed potatoes around the edge of the dish; sprinkle grated cheese over all. Slide under the broiler to brown, or place in a hot oven. Serves 6.

SHRIMP WIGGLE WITH MILK

3 tablespoons butter or margarine
3 tablespoons flour
2 cups warm milk
1 cup peas (cooked or canned)
1 can shrimp or 1 cup cooked shrimp
½ medium-sized onion, not sliced
salt and pepper to taste

Prepare a medium white sauce by melting the butter over direct heat and blending in the flour; cook and stir until smooth and well blended, adding milk gradually. Stir constantly. When this has thickened slightly, remove to a double boiler and add the peas (drained), the shrimp (cleaned of the black vein), and the onion. Allow to heat thoroughly 15 to 20 minutes. Remove the onion and season with salt and pepper. Serve very hot over crisp crackers. Serves 6 generously.

BAKED STUFFED MACKEREL

Select a mackerel weighing four or five pounds. Clean, rub salt inside and out, and stuff. Fasten together with a skewer or tie with string. Brush with melted fat and place in a baking pan.

Bake for 15 minutes in a very hot oven, 450° F. As it browns, reduce heat to 400° F. and bake for about 45 minutes longer. Serve with egg sauce and lemon slices. Serves 5 or 6.

PLAIN STUFFING

1 cup bread crumbs	½ teaspoon sage
½ cup melted butter or margarine	½ cup hot water
	½ onion, minced
¼ teaspoon salt	dash of pepper

Mix all together lightly with a fork.

EGG SAUCE

4 tablespoons butter	½ teaspoon salt
4 tablespoons flour	dash of pepper
2 cups scalded milk	2 hard-cooked eggs

Melt butter, add flour, and blend well. Pour over the scalded milk and cook until thick. Season. Cut the hard-cooked eggs in small pieces and add.

FISH BALLS

6 or 7 medium-sized potatoes

1 pint of finely picked salt fish (canned or packaged fish may be used)

2 eggs

1 tablespoon melted butter

pepper to taste

flour or cracker crumbs

Pare the potatoes and put in a kettle with salt fish on top. Cover with boiling water and boil ½ hour. Drain and mash together potatoes, fish, slightly beaten eggs, butter, and pepper. (If liked, a little grated onion is good.) Beat all together until light, and cool slightly. Make into balls and roll well in flour or cracker crumbs. Fry golden brown in very hot fat (385° F.) (Do not crowd when frying. Be sure fat is thoroughly heated.) This makes 14 small balls.

Note: When canned or packaged fish is used in this recipe, add the fish directly to the hot, drained potatoes and mash together with seasonings until light.

These fish balls may be prepared in advance, even to crumbing, ready to fry at the last minute.

CREAMED CODFISH IN POTATO RING

½ pound salt codfish

2 tablespoons butter

2 tablespoons flour

2 cups warm milk

4 hard-cooked eggs, sliced

4 cups well seasoned mashed potatoes

Freshen the codfish in cold water, drain, cover again with cold water, and bring to a boil. Drain and flake. Melt butter in a double boiler, add flour and blend well. Add milk and cook until thickened, stirring constantly. Add flaked fish and the eggs. Arrange the hot mashed potatoes around the edge of a serving platter or chop-plate and pour the creamed fish in the center. Serves 6. This Maine dish is simple, delicious and economical, since the eggs add quantity and nourishment. Paprika or chopped parsley may be added for color.

FINNAN HADDIE CASSEROLE

1 finnan haddie (1 to 1½ lbs.)
milk to cover fish
2 tablespoons butter
1 small green pepper (sweet), diced
1 medium onion, diced
4 tablespoons flour
dash of salt
2½ cups warm milk

Cut fish in 3 or 4 pieces, place in saucepan and cover with milk (skim milk is good). Place over low flame and let simmer until fish is ready to flake (about ½ hour.) While this is cooking, melt butter in another saucepan, add green pepper and onion and cook gently over fire about 10 minutes. Add flour and stir constantly until smooth and blended. Add salt and milk and cook until thickened, stirring constantly. Remove bones and skin from fish, then flake it and place in a buttered casserole. Pour the thick sauce over fish, sprinkle with paprika and buttered crumbs if desired, and bake in hot oven (400° F.) about 10 minutes.

FISH CHOWDER

¼ lb. salt pork, cubed
4 cups diced raw potatoes
1 teaspoon salt
3 lbs. fresh skinned haddock with bones in it

3 onions, sliced
1 can evaporated milk (13 oz.) or 1 cup rich milk, scalded
1 tablespoon butter
¼ teaspoon pepper

Fry the salt pork in the pot in which the chowder is to be made. Remove fried pork, put into the pot the onions, potatoes, and half the salt. Cover with hot water and cook until potatoes are tender, but not broken. Cut the fish into three pieces, and simmer in a separate pot to which the remaining salt has been added. (This is to keep the fish from breaking up.) When the fish is cooked, remove the bones, keeping the flesh in as large pieces as possible. Then put fish and strained fish stock (for flavor) into heated chowder dish. Add milk, butter, and pepper. Serves 5.

FISH HASH

Take equal parts of cold flaked fish and cold boiled potatoes, finely chopped; season with salt and pepper. Add salt sparingly, since pork fat often seasons sufficiently. Fry out salt pork, remove scraps, leaving enough fat in pan to moisten fish and potatoes. After thoroughly mixing fish and potatoes, put into hot fat in pan and cook until well browned, then turn and fold like an omelet.

Eating blueberries in Maine in summer is one of the essential freedoms, and to have them in one form or another for breakfast, luncheon, and dinner is perfectly permissible. Many people like to pick and eat them right off the bushes between meals. Thoreau did this when he visited Maine. It is not uncommon in the blueberry country to see signs reading:

"Blueberry Barren. Admission $1.00."

This means that by paying whatever fee is asked you may enter and pick all you want. If you have the patience and industry, you can gather berries enough to have blueberry pie, blueberry muffins, blueberry pancakes, blueberry pudding, and just blueberries submerged in cream. There is also the old New England combination of bread and milk and blueberries.

It is much easier, however, to buy the berries at a store or stand, and generally there is a plentiful supply, as blueberries grow more abundantly in Maine than anywhere else in the United States. Over sixty-five per cent of the nation's supply of this delicious fruit is grown in the state.

The first settlers along the coast could scarcely help noticing that where the timber had been cut off and the land burned over, blueberry vines or bushes sprang up in the thin, sandy soil, and produced amazingly fine crops of berries. It was as if nature in a compensatory mood were making up for the loss of the trees. Many stands of vines have yielded crops of far greater value than the original timber.

The settlers picked the berries for home consumption, eating them fresh in summer and drying supplies for winter use. It is curious that today this ancient method of preservation should have been revived. Experiments in blueberry dehydration have proved successful, and the new product has helped to expand the market.

Maine's blueberry belt extends along nearly the whole length of the seaboard, but most of the crop is grown at the easterly end, where there are vast stretches of blueberry barrens or plains. In mid-June the low bushes are covered with bell-shaped blossoms, and in midsummer the silvery-blue berries, each with its tiny crown, ripen under the Maine sun.

The berries prosper on the islands as well as on the mainland. Isle au Haut was famous for its "plums," as they called the berries, and people came from near and far to pick them. The "plummers," or pickers, lived on board their sailing craft, coming ashore in the daytime to gather the fruit.

Picking blueberries by hand is hard, slow work, but it is a long time since this method has been used by the owners of the blueberry barrens. Rakes not unlike those used on Cape Cod to harvest cranberries are used, and eight or nine men in the course of a few hours can pick thirty or forty bushels. Blowers are used to rid the berries of leaves and bits of vine picked up by the rakes, and the boxes of "blues" are trucked to the canneries, where they are weighed and dumped into conveyors.

Great strides have been made in processing blueberries. The old way was to cook the berries in a kettle, pour the fruit into tin cans, and then solder on the tops. There was no telling what you might find in a can of blueberries. Strange souvenirs of Maine used to turn up in them. Nowadays the berries are carefully sorted, cleansed, and while still fresh are placed in cans. Hot syrup is added to sweeten the berries, and the can, after a vacuum has been drawn, is sealed. The contents are then sterilized by cooking.

Flash freezing of the berries has also proved very successful. The cold pack method of placing the fruit in cold storage to freeze slowly did not work well owing to the formation of ice crystals which upon defrosting made the berries soggy.

Blueberries ask very little and give much. They

grow practically wild and require a minimum of cultivation, though to promote new growth the barrens are burned every third year. By dusting the fields with a poisonous compound the maggot, which was terribly destructive, has been expelled. Sea gulls have proved a nuisance because they love the berries and eat quantities of them. There is a popular legend that it is legitimate to shoot them in the blueberry country, though elsewhere on the Maine seaboard they are strictly protected.

The first fresh blueberry pie usually makes its appearance about the fifteenth of July. The women of Maine have been making them with such success for generations that blueberry pie is now a Maine institution. Perhaps because Maine is wonderful pie country it is also a great place for cheese. A lot is made there and much more is consumed. So cheese conscious are the people that I have known a rumor spreading through a town that a certain store had a particularly fine cheese to cause a run on the place. Lon Jewett, who kept the general store and post office at Head Tide, always had a good, ripe, tangy American cheese on hand, which went very well with blueberry pie.

With its fine foods and traditionally fine cooking, Maine is no place to go on a diet.

I T'S A N old Maine custom to be conscious of
the weather. For centuries the destiny of a large
proportion of the people was bound up with the
sea. Naturally they were deeply interested in the
weather, and watched closely for any indication
of changes that might affect them for better or
for worse. Through keen observation they developed a body of weather lore that proved very useful in determining future conditions, and a race of

prophets arose who could foretell the weather with amazing accuracy.

It was ignorance of the weather conditions normally prevailing along the coast that defeated the first attempt to found a settlement in Maine. There was a general feeling in England that New England winters were too cold for Englishmen. To prove that this was not true, a colony was planted at Popham at the mouth of the Kennebec River in 1607, the same year that Jamestown was settled. The expedition was well organized and equipped, but the first winter was one of extraordinary severity. None of the colonists had experienced anythink like it. They thought it was the usual kind of winter they could expect, and they did not care for it. It was nothing they had bargained for, and, discouraged by the ordeal and the death of their leader, they crowded on board the relief ship when it arrived and returned to England. This failure of the Popham colony gave New England a bad reputation which it took years to live down.

Fogs are the chief dread of the navigator on the Maine coast. Spells of foggy weather lasting, with brief intervals of respite, a week or more are not unknown, but they are not too common an experience of the region. Visibility seldom remains continuously low for protracted periods, and the records seem to indicate that this has always been pretty much the case. Yet in the past there has been enough to be troublesome. Fog, indeed, has played a muffled and sinister part in Maine history. In the early days the Indians took advantage of it to cover their attacks on the settlers, and in the days of sail it was the cause of most of the shipwrecks.

Summer is the foggy season, but just as there are wet summers and dry summers, so may there be years when fog is a rare or a frequent visitor. One redeeming feature of the Maine fogs is that when it is as thick as pea soup outside the bays, harbors, and rivers, it is often relatively clear inside, at least during the middle of the day. Because of the purity of the air the fogs are also white and clean. It is when the air contains impurities, such as smoke and soot, that the vapor particles become murky.

Fog is unpredictable stuff and may shut down without warning at any time. But there are certain omens which are indicative of its approach and withdrawal. Thus, whatever kind of day it may be, if a wisp of mist is observed hanging over the Camden hills or Mount Desert, it is fairly certain to be foggy the next day. If during a fog the barometric pressure drops below thirty, the lifting of the fog will soon follow. When a fog bank is visible offshore and it is calm during the ebb tide, then the fog will come in with the ensuing flood if the weather continues calm.

Every summer when fog is present on a lavish scale some visiting fogy writes to the local paper in praise of it. The line generally taken is that fog shuts out the world, giving one a restful interlude in which to meditate on life or anything else that pleases the fancy of the fog-bound one. It is also usually remarked that the clouds will surely break and the sun shine again upon this Utopia of ours.

There is, of course, a difference between mist and haze and fog, but the distinction is not too clearly defined. Mist curling up out of a valley in the early morning is a lovely sight. The purple haze of an Indian-summer day can give an effect of matchless beauty. But not so much can be said for fog, though I have known its cool dampness to be a welcome relief in hot weather. Winter vapor rising from the water is a curious phenomenon. When you see it you know it is really cold. It can obscure things all day long.

Fog seems to magnify small sounds, perhaps because we are unable to see clearly, and become more dependent on our sense of hearing. Yet one does not hear many bird notes in a fog, which apparently dampens their spirits. They become silent and less active and many stop feeding. The large numbers of small birds which used to die in gloomy city zoos and aviaries puzzled the keepers for some time, until it was discovered that they were starving to death. Switching on the lights saved them.

Birds are sometimes killed by flying into lighthouses during thick weather. Although they are able to keep to a certain line of flight at night, their wonderful directional sense seems to be affected by fog. They become disoriented, and it is then that they are apt to collide with the lights. Not many sea birds are destroyed in this way; it is usually the smaller land birds during the migratory periods that become casualties. Yet lighthouse keepers with whom I have talked have stated that the number of birds killed during storms and fogs is not very great. In clear weather the lights do not lure birds to their destruction.

Since time immemorial man has seen signs and portents in the behavior of birds, and some of these ancestral beliefs persist today. Here are some which were given to me by the wife of a Maine fisherman.

Sea gulls flying over the land indicate rain.

One crow flying alone is a sign of bad weather.

If crows fly in pairs, expect fine weather.

An unusual number of robins is a sign of rain.

If a rooster crows while perched on a fence or high place, it will clear. If he is on the ground, it doesn't count.

Blue jays call for rain.

Although bats are not birds, it is a sign of fair weather if they fly late at night.

To return for a moment to the fog. Silence is its usual accompaniment, although along the coast it inevitably brings into action the various navigation warnings—the bells, whistles, sirens, and horns—which continue day and night until the fog lifts. The foghorns differ in tone and in the time-spacing of the blasts to facilitate station recognition. Various types of apparatus are used which sound differently—reed horns, diaphragm horns, and diaphones. If a two-tone signal is used, the first part of the blast is high, the last part low. The so-called chime signal is produced by using units of duplex or triplex trumpets. Some foghorns are more powerful than others, so they differ in range of audibility, but they can be heard for long distances. Charles Campbell, the Portland bookseller, once told me that when the wind was right he could hear the Cape Elizabeth fog signal at his home ten miles away. One of the most dramatic sounds one can hear on the coast is the whistle of a steamer, anxious and questioning in the fog.

In the days before the lighthouse bells were mechanically operated, it must have been tedious ringing them by hand. At some lights the keepers enlisted the services of boys to sound the bell.

Many of the old books on navigation include a section devoted to weather prognostics deduced from the appearance of the sun, the moon, the stars, the sky and clouds, and rainbows. One such book published in 1732, which I looked at recently, is an heirloom in a Maine family whose members were for generations seafarers—the women as well as the men. If you have a weakness for rainbows, you will be interested in what the book has to say concerning them.

"The natural Signification of the Rainbow, is to fhew Rain paft or to come.

"The Rainbow appearing when it is Fair, is a Sign of Foul Weather; but a Rainbow appearing after Rain, fignifies Fair Weather: The Greener it appears, the more Rain; the more Wind, if it appears Redder. If it fhews very Light in the Blue Part, expect Fair Weather. If the Rainbow is feen before Noon, then the Rain is fpent; if at One or Two Afternoon, the Rain is near. A Rainbow in the Morning, is a Sign of Wet, (unlefs the Air abound with Moifture.) A Rainbow at Night, oppofite to the Moon, is a Sign of much Small Rain and Wind to follow. A Rainbow after long Rain, is Sign of Fair Weather, prefently. If Two Rainbows appear together, it is a Sign of Rain within Two or Three Days."

Interest in the weather even extended to the Bible, as witness the following predictions from the Scriptures, which appeared in an almanac of wide circulation in Maine a century ago.

"1st A cloud rising out of the west, foreshoweth rain. Luke XII. 54.

"2nd And when ye see the south wind blow, ye say there will be heat and it cometh to pass. Luke XII. 55.

"3rd When it is evening ye say, it will be fair
      weather, for the sky is red. Matt. XVI. 2.
"4th And in the morning, it will be foul weath-
      er today, for the sky is red and lowering.
      Matt. XVI. 3.
"5th South wind or great heat in the summer
      foretelleth whirlwinds. Job XXXVII. 9.
"6th Wind in the north predicteth cold weath-
      er. Job XXXVII. 9.
"7th Fair weather cometh out of the north. Job
      XXXVII. 22.
"8th The north wind driveth away rain. Prov.
      XXV. 23."

Maine weather vanes show great variety and
character. On the seaboard they often take the
form of fish and ships. Among the piscatorial vanes
the swordfish is perhaps the most popular. Whales
are also great favorites. Sea gulls and water birds
have frequently served as models, though they
seem to be outnumbered, even on the coast, by the
roosters, eagles, and occasional crows. A seagoing
farmer could with equal propriety adopt either a
rural or nautical style weather vane. Some of the
old wooden vanes were whittled at sea, to while
away the time on shipboard. The figurehead carvers near the shipyards sometimes turned their
hands to making weather vanes. Perhaps these artists were responsible for the most delightful of all

Maine vanes—those that represent the Angel Gabriel blowing his horn. These were once common, but are now rarely seen.

The church weather vanes are generally large and are mostly in the form of banners and arrows. Since they are usually painted or gilded it is often impossible to tell whether they are made of wood or metal. In January, 1949, the century-old weather vane atop the one hundred and twenty-five foot spire of the Congregational Church at Boothbay Harbor was damaged during a storm and had to be taken down. It was a six-foot arrow, thought to be of metal weighing a hundred or a hundred and fifty pounds. On the sloping edges of ancient stone spires one frequently sees architectural ornaments like curved foliage. These are crockets designed originally to give access to the weathercock. The wooden spire of the Boothbay Harbor church, however, is not equipped with these, and getting at the heavy vane, which seemed ready to fall, presented a problem. At length a rigger from one of the shipyards at East Boothbay climbed the steeple carrying an acetylene torch and was placing a rope around the vane when it suddenly came loose in his hand. But he had no trouble holding it, as the old weather vane was made of wood, not metal, and weighed comparatively little. Its length, it is supposed, was exactly that of the maker—six feet two inches.

Writers sometimes refer to nor'east gales, or a nor'easter, but perhaps it is worth noting that in the vicinity of Boothbay Harbor the fishermen call it a no'theast gale, or no'theaster, using the long sound of "o". This, I am told, is what the old-timers called it fifty years or more ago.

That was the period of the bearded sea captains, when a beard or throat whiskers were considered a protection against the weather. One of the most famous beards belonged to old Alec Adams. He had a luxuriant head of hair merging into a bushy beard which continued into his neck and by no means lessened as it bristled from his robust chest. People still remember the day he and his next-door neighbor, old Parnell, got into an argument and wielded pitchforks in the dusty road, only the intervention of their wives saving them from outright destruction.

A common sight along the coast used to be the hay schooners with their decks piled so high with baled hay that they looked top-heavy. The appearance of one of these schooners was taken by some people to be an infallible sign of rain. The story is told of one hay schooner which was lost in a peculiar manner. During a storm of wind and rain the canvas covering of the hay was blown away, and the unprotected hay became so waterlogged and heavy that the schooner turned turtle and sank.

TO HAVE A GENUINE SENSE
OF HUMOR

NEW ENGLAND was the cradle of American
wit and humor. For generations the Yankee ped-
dler was the country's stock comic character. The
earliest and widest known humorists were New
Englanders. They set the pattern that gave America
its distinctive brand of humor. And the native sons
of Maine played an important part in establishing
the tradition.

Of the Maine humorists, Artemus Ward is perhaps the best known. He wrote in one of his letters, "I was born in the State of Maine of parents. As an infant I abstracted a great deal of attention. The nabers would stand over my cradle for hours and say, 'How bright that little face looks! How much it nose!'"

His real name was Charles Farrar Browne. He was born in Waterford, April 26, 1834. When he was just entering his teens his father died and he was put to learning the printer's trade in Lancaster, New Hampshire. After a few years he returned to Maine to work for his older brother, Cyrus, who was editor of the *Norway Advertiser*. Then he went to Boston where for three years he was employed in a printing plant. That was the era of the roving journeyman printer and journalist, the man with ink, alcohol, and wanderlust in his veins. Young Browne followed his fortunes westward to Cincinnati, Toledo, and Cleveland. In Cleveland he went to work on the *Plain Dealer*, and it was while on the staff of this paper that he first began to write under the pen name of Artemus Ward. He invented the character of an itinerant and illiterate showman who wrote letters to editors in places where he wanted to exhibit. The first letter appeared in February, 1858, and was so well received that he followed it with a whole series. Newspapers all over the country were soon printing the letters of Artemus Ward. The following excerpt from one of them is typical.

"To the Editor of the ———

"Sir—I'm movin along—slowly along—down tords your place. I want you should rite me a letter, saying how is show bizzniss in your place. My show at present consists of three moral Bares, a Kungaroo (a amoozin little Raskal—t'would make you larf yerself to deth to see the little cus jump and squeal) wax figgers of G. Washington Gen. Tayler John Bunyan Capt. Kidd and Dr. Webster in the act of killin Dr. Parkman besides several miscellanyus moral wax statoots of celebrated piruts & murderers, &c., ekalled by few & exceld by none. Now Mr. Editor, scratch orf a few lines sayin how is the show bizniss down to your place. I shall have my handbills dun at your offis. . . .

"Respectively yures
"A. WARD.
"P.S. You scratch my back & Ile scratch your back."

The year following the appearance of the first of these letters found Artemus Ward in New York, a leading contributor to the comic periodical *Vanity Fair,* for which he wrote numerous humorous sketches and burlesque pieces. Many of these, with his letters, were collected and published in 1862 in *Artemus Ward: His Book,* which became a best seller.

Meanwhile, he had actually become a showman himself by appearing as a comic lecturer. He made his debut at New London, Connecticut, November 21, 1861. In his writing he depended a good deal for his humorous effect on the use of crazy spelling, which he could not do on the platform, but there was something more than that to his humor, and he was a hit. He was a lean young man with sandy hair, a full mustache, and a melancholy countenance. Stephen Leacock says his platform humor depended on his odd personality, his whimsical assumptions of distress and ignorance, and sudden flashes of interest fading into despair. He had, in short, all the eccentricities of a good comedian. His lecture was called "The Babes in the Wood," which needless to say had nothing to do with the unfortunate children in the forest.

Abraham Lincoln liked Artemus Ward's humor. At a critical period during the Civil War he read aloud to his Cabinet one of the humorist's pieces. This was the meeting of September 22, 1862. The piece was called "High-Handed Outrage at Utica." The President read it and laughed heartily, but he laughed alone as the Cabinet was not amused. Lincoln sighed at their silence and then read them the first draft of the Emancipation Proclamation. Here is Artemus Ward's "High-Handed Outrage," the reading of which outraged Lincoln's frumpish advisers.

"In the Faul of 1856, I showed my show in Utiky, a trooly grate sitty in the State of New York.

"The people gave me a cordyal recepshun. The press was loud in her prases.

"1 day as I was givin a descripshun of my Beests and Snaiks in my usual flowry stile what was my skorn & disgust to see a big burly feller walk up to the cage containin my wax figgers of the Lord's Last Supper, & cease Judas Iscarrot by the feet and drag him out on the ground. He then commenced to pound him as hard as he cood.

"'What under the son are you abowt,' cried I.

"Sez he, 'What did you bring this pussylanermus cuss here fur?' & he hit the figger another tremnjis blow on the hed.

"Sez I, 'You egrejus ass, that air's a wax figger— a representashun of the false 'Postle.'

"Sez he, 'That's all very well fur you to say, but I tell you, old man, that Judas Iscarrot can't show hisself in Utiky with impunerty by a darn site!' with which observashun he caved in Judasses hed. The young man belonged to 1 of the first famerlies in Utiky. I sood him, and the Joory brawt in a verdict of Arson in the 3d degree."

The country laughed when a theatrical manager in San Francisco wired Artemus Ward, "What will you take for forty nights in California?" and the comedian replied, "Brandy and soda." He went by way of the Isthmus of Panama and his tour was a great success. He returned by the overland route, lecturing in opera houses, gambling halls, and mining camps. At Virginia City, Nevada, he met a young man named Sam Clemens, who was to win fame as a humorist under the name of Mark Twain. At Salt Lake City he gathered material for his most celebrated lecture, "Artemus Ward Among the Mormons."

In June, 1866, he sailed for England. Few American writers have ever been so popular there. Only the last summer and winter of his short life were spent in England, but in those few months he won a host of friends. He contributed to *Punch* a series of articles which amused all England. He delighted the large audiences that filled the old Egyptian Hall in Piccadilly to hear him deliver his Mormon lecture, which was illustrated with panoramic pictures, and the lecturer also had the assistance of a pianist. He gave the lecture daily as long as his health permitted. He was afflicted with tuberculosis.

The friend who met him that summer on his arrival from America was shocked at his appearance. Instead of the fellow of infinite jest from whom he had parted in America the year before, he found Artemus "worn, wasted, and more grave than merry." But after a few hours' rest Artemus recovered somewhat and began to look around London. He visited the Tower of London and later made a pilgrimage to Stratford-on-Avon. It was his business to see the comic side of these places. They supplied the material for his *Punch* articles, which were written ostensibly by the unlettered showman whose imaginary adventures in the United States had brought renown to the author. In the account of his visit to the Tower of London is this passage:

"The Warder shows us some instrooments of tortur, such as thumbscrews, throat-collars, etc., statin that these was conkered from the Spanish Armady, and addin what a crooil people the Spaniards was in them days—which elissited from a bright-eyed little girl of twelve summers the remark that she tho't it *was* rich to talk about the crooilty of the Spaniards usin thumbscrews in a Tower where so many poor people's heads had been cut off. This made the Warder stammer and turn red.

"I was so pleased with the little girl's brightness that I could have kissed the dear child, and I would if she'd been six years older."

Artemus Ward considered that to have been invited to contribute to *Punch* was the finest compliment of his career.

To live up to his reputation as a humorist in private as well as in public must have taken considerable effort for this man of waning strength. He was personally extremely popular and was extensively entertained and not unnaturally was expected to show off at parties. He made his headquarters at the Savage Club, the rendezvous of the wits and bohemians of the day, and it was inevitable perhaps that in such company he should drink more than was good for him. At length in January he had to give up lecturing and go away for his health. He went to Jersey for a while, which seemed to benefit him, but on his return he was unable to stand the strain of the journey to London, and remained in Southampton, where he died on March 6, 1867, at the age of thirty-three. In May his body was taken to America for burial at Waterford.

Artemus Ward was not the first Maine humorist to gain distinction. Seba Smith (1792-1868), who was born in a log cabin in Buckfield, won fame as a homespun philosopher and political satirist under the name of Major Jack Downing. Though his early education was somewhat meager, he made a brilliant record at Bowdoin College from which he was graduated in 1818. He became assistant editor of the Portland *Argus*, and in 1829 launched the first daily newspaper in Maine, the Portland *Courier*. Early in the following year the first of the famous letters of Major Jack Downing of Downingville began to appear in the *Courier*. It was the Andrew Jackson era and the satirical Yankee humor of the letters caught the popular fancy. Stephen Leacock says that Smith "led the way for a host of homely

philosophers and critics from Sam Slick and Hosea
Biglow to Mr. Dooley and Will Rogers."

Another popular Maine-born humorist was Bill
Nye, who was christened Edgar Wilson Nye. He
was born in 1850 in Shirley, a tiny town not far
from Moosehead Lake. His family was very poor
and when he was two years old they emigrated to
Wisconsin. Like Seba Smith and Artemus Ward,
Bill Nye became a journalist. He left Wisconsin in
1876 and went to Laramie, Wyoming, where he
did some work for the Laramie *Daily Sentinel*. His
career might have ended that year had he accepted
the offer of the San Francisco *Chronicle* to go as
correspondent with General Custer, but as he explained later, difficulty in checking his trunks delayed him, so he missed the battle of the Little Big-
horn and Custer's last stand. It was not long before
Bill Nye's amusing letters of current comment attracted wide attention. In these he did what bat-
talions of columnists are engaged in doing today.
In 1886 he joined the New York *World*, but during
the lecture season he traveled widely in the United
States and Canada, drawing crowds of people eager
to make the closer acquaintance of the man who
had made them laugh. For almost twenty years
he wrote and lectured, and then in 1896, at the age
of forty-six, Bill Nye died.

Fashions in humor change and the methods used
by Seba Smith, Artemus Ward, and Bill Nye in the

last century are now outmoded, but these brilliant
men have their place in American history because
they added to the gaiety of the nation and set the
pattern for their successors in the same field.

The New England country store was a great forc-
ing ground of native humor. It was here that the
village wits and wags assembled. Men went there
as to a club for relaxation and entertainment. This
was especially the case in Maine, which went
dry in 1846, so it did not have the taverns that other
parts of New England had, where men could gather
and imbibe good cheer in a congenial atmosphere.
The general store was about the only place in
which the pothouse Platos of Maine could congre-
gate.

Nathaniel Hawthorne's uncle, Richard Man-
ning, kept a general store near Sebago Lake, and
when as a boy Nathaniel visited his uncle he liked
to listen to the stories told by the men who gathered
at the store. He could appreciate a joke even when
it was at his uncle's expense. An entry in his diary
reads: "Captain Britton from Otisfield was at Uncle
Richard's today. Not long ago Uncle brought here
from Salem a new kind of potatoes called Long
Reds. Captain Britton had some for seed and Uncle
asked how he liked them. He answered, 'They yield
well, grow very long; one end is very poor and the
other good for nothing.' I laughed about it after he
was gone, but Uncle looked sour, and said there

was no wit in his answer and the saying was stale.
It was new to me and his way of saying it very
funny."

Without humor, life in many remote communities would have been pretty dull. It gave a needed
fillip to existence in these places, and the tendency
was to give it free play. People developed the habit
of looking at life with amused detachment. It was
an individual outlook that came naturally to them.
It was a humorous attitude that entered their
speech and figured largely in their lives. And it is
still preserved as a living tradition in Maine.

This hereditament of humor is characterized by
understatement rather than by exaggeration, and
is often accompanied by a certain soberness of de-
meanor or delivery that heightens the effect. Like
the man Hawthorne overheard in his uncle's store,
Maine people can say things in an amusing way.
Manner, tone, accent, and picturesque figures of
speech all play a part.

Once when I was talking with a man he said of
one of his relatives, "He was cut out to be a deacon,
but the scissors slipped." It was an apposite remark
at which I laughed since I knew the character to
whom he referred, but much of the piquancy of
the observation lay in the way he said it, and this
I find impossible to reproduce in words.

For the same reason scant justice can be done to
the following incident. One rainy day a woman of

my acquaintance, a summer visitor to Maine, who was anxious to go somewhere as soon as there was a break in the weather, went down to the wharf and asked a prehistoric-looking captain there if he thought it would clear. The old salt looked over the whole sky very carefully, meditated for a moment, and then said, "Don't see why it won't. It always has."

Theodore Roosevelt, who liked to fish in Maine, was fond of telling of the wet spring he was there. While proceeding along a rocky road he said to his guide, "How do you tell the roads from the river?"

"No beaver dams in the roads," was the prompt reply.

Very apt was the description one man gave of the Yankee genius of his neighbor. "Why, he could make money on a half-tide ledge."

Maine has had its practical jokers. Barney Beal of Beal's Island, a man of giant stature and fabulous strength, whose arms when he sat in a captain's chair dragged on the floor, was one of these. There was only one man on the coast who was his equal and that was Ruggles Mitchell of Harrington. Uncle Rug sometimes sailed to Boston with Barney, and the pair through sheer excess of spirits would clean up whole streets of men, first one and then the other taking the lead in maltreating everyone who crossed their path. They were even capable of knocking down horses that got in their way.

While understatement is the hallmark of most Maine humor, exaggeration also plays a part. Story telling is one of the oldest forms of entertainment, and in many isolated Maine villages it was a favorite pastime. Stories which perhaps were originally founded on fact were in time improved and built up into the loftiest kind of tall tale. These yarns achieved a certain measure of circumstantiality by being set in familiar localities and by the use of local names. From a simple story of coon hunting probably comes the tall tale of the man who treed one of these animals and was taking aim at it when the coon cried, "Don't shoot, deacon! I'll come down."

Maine people dearly love stories concerning out-of-state visitors. Such a story, for example, as that of the stranger being shown around a town who remarked to his guide on the extraordinary number of elderly people in the place. "Seems as if everybody we meet is old," he said.

"Yes, the town has lots of old folks," the guide admitted.

"I see you have a cemetery over there," remarked the stranger.

"Yes," was the laconic answer, "we had to kill a man to start it."

Embedded in the Maine vernacular are many

colorful expressions. If a man is blue he is often "bluer'n a whetstone," or he may be "hotter'n love in hayin' time," or "hotter'n a red barn." He may not need a thing "any more than a dog needs two tails," though he may swear "by the Great Horn spoon" that he does. The night may be "black as zip," or a thing as "slick as schoolmarm's leg."

Nautical terms are commonly used along the seaboard, which gives a strong seasoning of salt to most coastal talk. An old seagoing farmer was heard to say, "Drive the cow into the barnyard, son, and I'll dock her." Again, when the reins were slack on the dashboard, "Haul in the mainsheet!" And the sea is in the speech of the women as well as in that of the men. The saltiest vocabulary I ever heard was that of Ma Peasley, famed social worker of the Maine Seacoast Mission. She it was who made the amusing remark when the present mission boat was launched, "I hope she won't be a holy roller."

The first land in the United States on which the sun shines in the morning is Mount Katahdin in Maine. From this has come the saying that the state is the place where they pry up the sun, a proverb that has given rise to humorous drawings like the one at the head of this chapter.